Contents

Forward

There are great difficulties about writing true crime stories especially about murder as there is an importance in keeping them as accurate to the truth as possible yet protecting the innocent. This story is based on the true facts about the four cases reported, but with no victims to say what happened and offenders who did not admit or explain their crimes, some of the fine detail has been added by me to make for better reading.

I have given my thoughts and views on how the crimes occurred, this is based on the evidence gathered during the investigations and my interpretation of what the evidence most likely indicates.

I do not apologise for the graphic detailed account of these attacks on the victims as the facts are accurate and demonstrate the viciousness, callousness and depravity of the offenders. The facts were obtained from the original crime files now currently stored in the Major Crime archive stores based at Avon and Somerset Police Headquarters, Portishead and directly from my own memories having worked on the cases. I lived the jobs for many months and spoke directly to people connected to the case, giving me an insight into the effect that the crime had on the victim's family.

The names of some people in the cases have been changed to protect their identity and to preserve their privacy. The murder victims' details are correct. The cases can be found on the internet as some facts are already in the public domain due to reporting of the court cases.

If having read the book you disagree with my interpretation of the evidence, then feel free to form your own opinion as the only people who really know the truth are the victims and those who committed the crime.

CW01502135

Background

I left Frome college just before my 18th birthday, I had come away with two 'A' levels and 11 'O' levels, but I had already decided what my career was to be. My family believe that I probably chose the police because my uncle Steve was an Inspector with the Northamptonshire police, working in their control room. My grandfather had also been in the Northamptonshire police, having retired as a Chief Inspector in charge of their scenes of crime department, specialising in photographic evidence and fingerprints. So, there was a tradition of police officers in the family, and I had grown up with tales of crimes and police investigations that fascinated me. I knew I was not interested in control room work or even scenes of crime, but crime investigation was always my target even before I joined.

It was necessary to be 18 ½ years old before starting in the police so I found a job for 8 months as a handyman for a local sack merchant.

On Monday the 7th of March 1977, I started my police training in Kings Weston House, Bristol followed by 10 intensive weeks in Chantemarle regional training centre, Dorset, learning about the law and police procedures. I was posted to 'B' Division, Broadbury Road police station, which was in the heart of Knowle

West, one of the largest council estates in Bristol. Having grown up in the town of Frome, I found the move to the big city an eye opener and the crime levels for me seemed unbelievably high. I had always been good with remembering names and faces and soon got to know most of the local criminals. Whenever anyone was circulated as wanted for a crime, you could bet that I would have a good idea where they were likely to be hanging out or who they would be with. I soon got the reputation of being one of the best thief takers on the district and there was rarely a two or three day period when I had not arrested someone for some crime.

I was determined that someday I was going to become a Detective in order to investigate the more serious crimes, but I knew it was necessary to learn my craft by spending several years in uniform first.

In 1983, the Avon and Somerset police put out an advert for any person interesting in applying to join the CID and I was quick to apply. Following an interview with three senior officers, I was one of 10 people successful, and I was posted to Bishopsworth Police station also on 'B' Division but located in Hartcliffe, another large council estate. It was there that I learnt my detective skills and it was soon apparent that I had the necessary inquisitive mind, dogged determination and 'can do' attitude required to be a good detective. I soon got to investigate very complex cases such as serious frauds, burglaries, robberies, and serial offenders. It was also whilst at Bishopsworth that I got my first taste of being part of a murder investigation team.

One of the ways to get selected to work on a murder enquiry is to have a specialist skill so in 1984 I asked to go on an Exhibits Officer's course. An Exhibits Officer learns about searching crime scenes for evidence. They work alongside trained search teams who normally carryout the actual searching. The exhibits officer supports experienced scenes of crime officers so they need to understand how to read a crime scene and how to recover minute trace evidence. A crime scene is secured by the first officer attending the scene to ensure that no evidence is inadvertently destroyed. The exhibits officer records every single exhibit that is seized and ensures that it is packaged up correctly, stored correctly in order that forensic scientists have the maximum chance of recovering evidence to prove the offence.

An item for example, of wet or blood-stained clothing cannot be stored in a plastic bag as it would become mouldy very quickly and prevent scientists being able to obtain blood grouping or in later years DNA. The wet item needs to be carefully dried in a sterile environment before securing and labelling it in strong paper bags. An item soaked in some form of accelerant would be packaged in a nylon bag because this can prevent the escape of the volatile fumes which you are hoping the forensic scientist would find during their examination. Special packaging for knives and sharp objects is required so the item won't pierce the packaging and contaminate the exhibit. Lots of exhibits must be preserved for fingerprinting as well as forensic testing and it is important to know which examination comes first and how storage may affect results. Do you freeze an item, store it in a fridge or store it at room temperature? You need to know or forensic results can be lost.

I relished the challenge of this new role, knowing that I would get to work closely with other experts in their field. I would be attending many post-mortems where pathologists would dissect the body of the deceased to establish the cause of death. Dr Hugh White became my favourite pathologist as he would spend the time to show me why he was able to reach his conclusions. He would slice through a mark on the victim's flesh and be able to tell if it was a bruise that occurred before death or if it was simply livor mortis, referring to the pooling of blood in the lower portion of the body after death. Livor mortis results in dark purple discoloration of the skin and can help show if a body has been moved after death, the position of the livor mortis indicates how the deceased was originally lying after death.

Having completed the exhibits officer's course, I was soon chosen to carryout exhibits officer duties on a murder investigation. That murder is the subject of the first case I want to lead you through.

The Murder of Roy Page 1985

Chapter 1:

The Crime

It was the 18th of July 1985, Roy Page was sixty-one years old, he ran a corner tobacconist and sweetshop at 158, St John Lane Bedminster, Bristol and had done so since 1975. The shop was quite run-down with chipped and peeling paint on all the woodwork, even the name PAGE painted across the shop window was peeling badly. Roy had been a widower since 1982 and lived alone in the private residential area at the back of the shop. He was well known and well liked in the area due to his friendly nature, always having time for a chat with friends and neighbours who would pop in the shop for general groceries and cigarettes. Roy was the type of shop keeper who had everything in his shop and if you couldn't find what you wanted, he would make sure he would get the item for your next visit.

Roy Page's shop at 158, St Johns Lane Bedminster,Bristol

The clutter inside Roy Page's shop

Ever since Roy's wife Joan had died, Roy's family had worried about him looking after himself and had rallied around to care for him, even his 86-year-old mother would cook him daily meals and his sister Shirley would attend weekly to do all his cleaning. Thursday the 18th of July 1985 was no different. Shirley had already been round and tidied up, she noticed that he had yet again left his safe door open, and that money was clearly on display to anyone visiting the shop. Shirley closed the safe and reminded him to be more careful then left at about 4:15pm.

What was not known was that earlier that morning a man had travelled from Port Talbot in Wales to Temple Meads railway station in Bristol. He headed straight to the Horfield area in the north of the city. He was quite distinctive being about 6'2" tall, dark haired and heavily built, wearing headphones, and carrying some type of electronic device which was connected to an earpiece that was protruding from his ear. He was dressed in dark blue overalls.

He was seen on at least three occasions pacing up and down the street and seemed to focus his attention on tobacconists and sweetshops, occasionally speaking to members of the public and giving the impression that he was working for the gas board and looking for a gas leak. It was noted that he spoke with a noticeable Welsh accent. By the afternoon, he had moved down to the Bedminster area and was seen outside or very near Roy Page's shop. He called at several addresses in the area and again claimed to be a gas official looking for gas leaks.

Maureen and Elizabeth Gerrish were two elderly sisters who lived in nearby Hill Avenue and at about 4:00pm that afternoon, their doorbell rang. They opened the door to the bogus gasman who enquired if they had any gas leaks. They had no leaks but believed that a friend of theirs had, so they directed the man to a Mrs Perkins a few doors away in Almorah Road. Just before he left, Elizabeth noticed that the man's overalls had come undone and that he was wearing white underpants with thin blue piping along the waistband. I mention this small point now as it will become more significant later.

Mrs Perkins had indeed been concerned about a possible gas leak in her kitchen and when the man arrived, she invited him inside to investigate. He told her that he had found a leak but had no equipment with him to repair it. He requested a glass of water as he claimed to feel unwell and having gulped it down quickly, he hurriedly left not even switching her gas off at the mains.

Roy Page's shop was on the corner of Almorah Road and St John's Lane, so it is believed that the bogus gas man went straight there next. Two paperboys claimed to have seen him sometime between 4:30pm and 5:00pm and he appeared to be arguing with Roy outside his shop.

Shortly after 5:00pm, a woman walking opposite the shop saw a man fitting the description follow Roy into his shop. Mrs Martina

Allan was Mr Page's last known customer at 5:20pm and the three items she purchased were recorded on his till roll. The next possible sighting of the offender was at about 6:15pm, when a man walking home from work saw someone coming out of the side door to the shop. The description matched all the others, heavily built, dark hair, wearing glasses, but this time, he was without overalls although was thought to be carrying them under his arm.

About ninety minutes later, a friend and neighbour of Roy, Tom Coles, called at the shop to buy cigarettes but found the shop door locked. This was most unusual as whenever Roy had to leave the shop, he would always leave a notice to say he would be back in a few minutes. Ten minutes passed and there was still no sign of Roy. Tom knew that Roy was a diabetic and worried that he was perhaps collapsed ill inside the shop. Tom returned home and tried to telephone Roy but got no answer. When Tom returned to Roy's shop, quite a crowd had gathered outside. People were hammering on the door and shouting through the letterbox, but there was no response. A few minutes later, Roy's son Brian arrived and went to the rear of the premises to check the back door which he found locked. All the windows were closed and the curtains drawn, which Brian knew was very unusual as his father never drew the curtains.

Sensing that something was seriously wrong, Brian flagged down a passing police patrol car.

The police officers forced open the shop doors and were immediately met with the smell of gas. Inside, they found Roy lying slumped half in and half out of the hall cupboard under the stairs. Roy was clearly dead; he had been beaten severely around the head and had a piece of material forced down his throat. After making Brian leave the house, one of the police officers turned off the gas at the mains as every gas appliance in the house appeared to have been turned on, fortunately the pilot light on the gas cooker had gone out, if it hadn't, there would most likely have been a gas explosion. The officer then stood outside to preserve the scene and to await the attendance of other officers.

Very soon an ambulance arrived, followed by a police surgeon to confirm that Roy Page was deceased. The scene was then guarded to await detectives to take over the investigation.

I had worked a full day from 8:00am till 4:00pm and had only been home for about one hour when the telephone rang. The police control room had been asked by the DCI to contact me and request that I attend the scene of a murder to carry out exhibits officer duties. This was something that I had recently trained for but never done before. I was required to dress up in a white paper suit to avoid the possibility of any forensic contamination. I was at the scene to take possession of any exhibits that the forensic scientists or scenes of crime officer believed could be evidence. I was back at work and down at the murder scene by

8:00pm to await the arrival of scientists and the pathologist.

The forensic examination of the scene revealed very few clues. There was a broken table leg that had one end wrapped tightly in a piece of paper. The paper was actually a bag from the local chemist and enquiries showed that Roy Page regularly used the chemist to obtain his prescriptions. The table leg showed traces of Mr Page's blood and hair, so it was no doubt the murder weapon used to beat him. Near to the body, a piece of an old hearing aid or earpiece was found, which did not appear to belong to Roy Page. The daily takings of the shop were missing along with other cash, which together were estimated to be about £1,050 along with the contents of Mr Page's savings tin amounting to about £600, so initial indications pointed towards the motive for the murder as being robbery. The scenes of crime examination revealed numerous fingerprints but most of these were eliminated as belonging to Roy Page himself or known family members or friends. The two outstanding marks were to cause the team a lot of hard work. These consisted of one mark on the edge of the exterior side door and one on the outside of the lounge window at the rear of the premises. The mark on the door was identified three months later as being from a police officer who had attended at the scene just to have a quick look, he had never declared the fact that he had been there, which is why it took so long to identify it. The mark on the window was eventually identified as being the window fitters who had last touched the glass two years previously.

Roy's killer had been careless leaving behind the two vital clues at the crime scene. The first being the grey earpiece from a type of headphones used to listen to a Walkman or a transistor radio. This find indicated that the offender could well be the bogus gas official that the house-to-house team had learnt about.

Duplicate earpiece found during investigation

The second clue was much more damning. This was the empty chemist's bag that was wrapped around a broken chair leg and was covered in blood. The scene of crime officer could make out a partial fingerprint in blood on the chemist's bag and was sure that in their lab they would be able to enhance the fingerprint and then potentially identify the offender.

The chemist's bag was found to contain a prescription in Roy's name that had only recently been collected from the chemist. A fingerprint in blood on this bag had to be either Roy's print or the offender's.

An incident room was set up at Broadbury Road police station and Detective Superintendent Lew Clark was identified to head up the investigation as SIO, he had a deputy from the B Division CID office, Detective Inspector Bryan Saunders. Lew Clark was very experienced and had led many murder enquiries, he also had a background of working in the force press office.

It is normal practice that house-to-house enquiries are made in the vicinity of serious crimes. This is often a good source of information and was again going to prove to be invaluable. Maureen and Elizabeth Gerrish and Mrs Perkins were approached and supplied details of the man they had seen acting suspiciously in the area.

They gave detailed accounts and statements about the caller to their home addresses, a man claiming to be a gas board official and wishing to check their gas supply. This was a well-known means for burglars to gain access to properties to steal items but none of these witnesses had any property stolen. They were able to describe the man as being 6'2" tall, 35 years old, of heavy build with short dark hair, wearing a one-piece blue boiler suit and he spoke with a strong Welsh accent. They spoke about him walking around with some device held in his hand that he was waving from side to side apparently trying to detect something. The device was connected by a wire to an earpiece. Lew Clark was convinced that the man described was the offender for the murder of Roy, especially since an earpiece had been located inside Roy's house, which could not be accounted for by his family. Lew made the decision to circulate the description nationwide.

The witnesses each compiled photofit impressions of the man and the best of these was circulated in a hope of identifying who he was. The gas board had been unable to identify the man and they stated that none of their workers had been in the vicinity.

Lew Clarke had no doubt that the bogus gas official was the person responsible for the murder of Roy Page and that he was a burglar who had entered the shop to steal property. Whether his accent was genuine or one put on to throw us off the scent would need to be established. Research of all known burglars was carried out both with and without links to Wales but nothing relevant was found. The MO indices were also checked but no other crimes could be linked.

As time went on, it was discovered that the offender had stolen not only a quantity of cash from the premises but once the family had access to the building, they claimed that also missing was a cream-coloured purse along with a hairbrush which was part of a mirror and brush set.

The local press all gathered outside the shop asking questions. When the scene examination was complete, they requested to film the premises for the regional news, and I was asked to pretend to be searching or examining something in the main shop to make the filming more interesting. The following day, I saw myself on the local news and reporters described me as a forensic scientist busily searching for clues. (You can never believe what you hear on the media!)

I returned to Broadbury Road police station at about 5:00am and had about 100 exhibits to register and store away. Items such as the earpiece, table leg and paper bag had to be sent to HQ for specific fingerprint treatment as soon as possible. I found myself working right through the night.

The next morning, I attended at the post-mortem, where the pathologist confirmed that Roy had received several blows to the head from a blunt object and that the cause of his death was trauma to the head. The pathologist could not rule out the table leg as the weapon used.

I didn't get back home until gone10:00pm that night.

This murder investigation was before the introduction of the Home Office Large Major Enquiry System (HOLMES), a computerised system for managing major investigations, so I was required to use a series of index cards to record my exhibits. The table leg for example would result in a card being created under the heading 'Table Leg', a separate card under the heading 'Weapons', a card headed 'Blood' and a card headed 'Exhibits from scene'. The index cards would be updated regarding any forensic results, any person shown the exhibit or handling the exhibit, any movement of the exhibit and any actions raised for enquiries regarding that exhibit. By the conclusion of the investigation, all 700 exhibits in the case had to be recorded in this manner on index cards and they formed part of the 'carousel indexing paper recording system' that were used in murder investigations.

There were indexers employed to maintain index cards relating to people, suspects, vehicles, addresses, locations, house-to-house and various categories bespoke to the investigation.

I had discussions with the forensic scientists and the fingerprint experts to decide what more detailed forensic testing was required to be carried out on the main exhibits. The earpiece was firstly examined for fingerprints, but no useful impressions were found on it. As this item had belonged to the offender, it was also sent for forensic examination in case any blood grouping could be carried out on it. Unfortunately, no worthwhile forensic evidence was found on this exhibit. Actions were raised for enquiries to be made all over the country to find out the origin of the earpiece in a hope it could lead to the offender. I travelled to London and was shown hundreds of different earpieces at numerous manufacturers before I finally identified a similar one. The earpiece was simply an old-fashioned earpiece that was no longer in circulation. If only DNA had existed then, there is little doubt they would have found DNA on this item as it had spent a large part of the day stuck in the offender's ear.

The broken table leg came from a table in Roy's house and was smashed during the murder, it had not been brought to the scene by the offender. This item was forensically examined and fingerprinted. It was confirmed as the murder weapon due to fragments of the victim's skin and hair found stuck in the wood in blood and the shape of the table leg matched marks left of the deceased's body. No fingerprints were found on the table leg.

Broken table leg

The chemist's paper bag was treated with chemicals and this improved the fingerprints that had been visible to the naked eye. It was clear from the way the bag was folded that it had been wrapped around the table leg, possibly to stop the offender's grip slipping in the blood and possibly to avoid leaving fingerprints on the weapon.

The rules and standards in 1985 stated that for a fingerprint expert to make an identification of a fingerprint, it was necessary to find 15 matching characteristics between the impression found at a crime scene and the fingerprints of a suspect. Fortunately for the police, those same rules and standards also stated that when two separate crime scene impressions are found on the same exhibit, the fingerprint expert can make a positive identification with a suspect's fingerprint if at least 10 matching characteristics can be found on each of the scene marks.

Fingerprint Characteristics

When the partial marks found on the chemist bag were examined by the expert, he was only able to find 10 characteristics on each mark. This meant that should a suspect be identified; it may be possible to prove that the suspect's fingerprints matched the marks in blood on the chemist's bag. It was also possible to search nationwide to identify if the prints matched any fingerprints already held by the police. This was not a simple process as it would be nowadays, there were no computers to carry out the searches, it would have to be done by fingerprint experts around the country. They would check any fingerprints held from burglars, robbers, and violent offenders to see if they had a match. No match was found nationally so it was likely our offender had never provided his fingerprints in the past. All the members of staff from the chemist and even staff from the manufacturers of the bags had their fingerprints taken for elimination but the impressions remained unidentified.

The enquiry had been very successful. It had been established what the murderer looked like, how he committed the crime, and all that was now needed was to put a name to the face. The fingerprint would hopefully do the rest. The Welsh accent could have been put on by the offender, so no one was eliminated due to not being Welsh.

Enquiries had also shown that our offender had attempted to carry out a similar burglary offence in a separate corner shop in another area of Bristol earlier in the day but investigations into that crime had not revealed any additional evidence.

Crimewatch UK was one of the most successful television programmes of its type to have ever been broadcast on UK television, it was a live show that televised crime reconstructions, showed CCTV, and had general appeals for evidence in cases where the police were drawing a blank at solving them. It invited viewers to call in with any information they may have concerning the crime. The aim of the programme was, not for people to offer their own wild theories as armchair detectives, but to call in if they could genuinely help by providing information on a featured crime. The public then telephoned in their information, either to the studio number or to the separate police incident room number dealing with the case in question.

Crimewatch UK was still a relatively new idea in 1985 having only run for one year but it had produced its successes. Subsequently, some of the most notorious crimes in British criminal history, such as the murder of Liverpool toddler James Bulger, the arrest and imprisonment of Michael Sams for the 1992 murder of Julie Dart and the kidnapping of estate agent Stephanie Slater, were solved as a direct result of information stemming from Crimewatch UK appeals.

Police forces across the UK jumped at the chance to have their appeals broadcast to a nationwide audience. But back in its early years, it didn't always have this appeal to the police. The police had a mistrust for the media and tended to avoid them at all costs. Lew Clark however, with his press office background had the foresight to request their assistance and this would prove to be the key to solving the case. Crimewatch records still report that one of its earliest success stories was the 1985 case of the "Bogus Gasman of Bristol."

Following Lew's request, Crimewatch UK stepped in. The show's researcher had seen appeals about Roy's murder in local press so already knew the basic story. Roy's family gave permission, and it was not long before filming started on a reconstruction.

On the 29th of August 1985, just six weeks after Roy's murder, twelve million people nationwide watched the reconstruction and heard Lew Clark appeal for information. Surely someone would recognise the man from the photofits or have an idea who was responsible.

Lew Clark was left disappointed because by the end of the evening there had been surprisingly few calls, with only one of significance. The caller, who lived in Bedminster had been away on holiday at the time that the case had been broadcast locally, she called to say that at about 5:15pm on the day of the murder she had visited Roy's shop to buy sweets for her daughter. She found the shop closed and when peering through the glass doors of the shop, she suddenly saw a man appear near the counter whose description matched that of the bogus gasman. The man had placed his hands against his cheek and mouthed the words, "He's asleep". Although this was important fresh evidence, because the woman had seen the killer at the crime scene, it brought police no nearer to catching him. It looked as though Crimewatch UK was going to fail on this occasion.

A week after the Crimewatch programme was broadcast, there was a new turn of events. On Friday the 6th of September, the bogus gasman took a day trip down to the south coast of England to Portsmouth. He was not someone that had ever bothered to watch Crimewatch, and he was seemingly unaware that millions of people had seen him portrayed in a TV reconstruction just one week earlier. He began to behave much the same way as he had in Bedminster on the day of Roy's murder. He was dressed the same and repeated the pattern of visiting small shops in the city's Fratton district. He wandered around the shops in Chichester Road for a while, lingering by the door and acting strangely.

Thirty minutes later, he was seen further down Chichester Road loitering outside a small newsagent shop. The witness who saw him, Stephen Harfield, was driving past and stopped the car to watch the man's behaviour.

Stephen had seen the Crimewatch reconstruction and after watching the suspicious behaviour for a few minutes, decided to call the police from a nearby public telephone box. He was one of six people in Portsmouth that day to ring the police and report the bogus gasman acting suspiciously.

Colin Weaver had also seen the reconstruction and something triggered his memory when he saw the man. He followed him into a local park, trailing him from a distance. Colin watched the bogus gasman wander over to a mound at the side of a playground, sit down and lay back basking in the warm September sun. Thinking that the man would stay there for a while, Colin went to the nearest telephone box and called the police.

Police Constable Hamilton from Portsmouth police station was sent to a call of a man acting suspiciously and found this man sat in the park. PC Hamilton could not believe his eyes because he too had seen Crimewatch UK on the previous Friday night and here was a man 6'2" tall, 35 years old, heavy build, short dark hair and wearing a one-piece blue overall. He was holding a Sony Walkman with earphones. It was like he was watching the reconstruction once again but in real life. When PC Hamilton asked the man his name, "Clive Richards" came the reply in a broad Welsh accent. Richards was searched and was in possession of some rubber gloves, a Walkman, a pair of white underpants with blue piping around the waistband, a heavy iron bar and a sheath knife. Richards happily admitted why he was carrying such weapons, claiming that these were for his own protection whilst he was carrying out his surveys. PC Hamilton was, by this time, convinced that they had the right man, and telephoned the Broadbury Road incident room. Lew Clark had very little to ponder and instructed that Clive Richards be arrested on suspicion of the murder of Roy Page.

The investigating team Deputy Senior Investigating Officer, Detective Inspector Bryan Saunders, journeyed down on a two-hour drive from Bristol to Portsmouth. All the while he was thinking, 'Is this too good to be true? This man matched the description from witnesses perfectly'. Upon arrival, he was struck by the items found in Richards' bag, the underpants matched the description of pants described by one of the Gerrish sisters. When Bryan heard Richards speak, he could not fail to pick up the strong Welsh accent.

But for Bryan Saunders, he became convinced that he had his killer in front of him, when immediately after arresting him on suspicion of the murder of Roy Page, Richards began to sweat profusely and ask for water exactly as Mrs Perkins had described the bogus gasman as doing. Richards kept gulping from a bottle of water all the way back to Bristol, denying that he had killed Roy Page and maintaining that he hadn't even been in Bristol on the day Roy Page was murdered.

Clive Richards had no previous convictions, so his fingerprints had never been taken before. Once the police had his fingerprints, they were matched to the two partial marks found on the paper bag that had been wrapped around the murder weapon. The fingerprint expert was able to match 10 characteristics from each mark to Clive Richards' fingerprints and because both impressions were on the same exhibit (the chemist's bag), this was considered as compelling evidence that should stand up in court. These facts were put to Richards, but he insisted that he had not been to Bristol for 20 years. Even when all three witnesses identified him at an ID parade, Richards would not change his story.

Enquiries made into Richards' movements following the murder showed that he went to London and exchanged up £500 into American dollars and then caught a train home to Port Talbot. Richards exchanged the money back to bank of England notes in Port Talbot thus losing out on the exchange on both occasions. Was this a way of changing up 'dirty money'? He explained his new-found wealth to his parents by saying he had been paid in American dollars by an old acquaintance for some work he was going to do but could not explain to the police why he had gone to London to purchase dollars.

Chapter 2:

The Suspect Clive Richards

So, what did we find out about Clive Richards? He was born in Port Talbot in Wales in 1950 and although he had an extremely high IQ, had left school without qualifications. He remained living at home with his parents, brother and sister. His family ran a fruit and veg business which was bringing in a steady income. They used him to drive a van laid out as a mobile shop taking the produce to customers. Clive had been encouraged by his parents to branch out the business, by expanding the range of stock in the shop and to include sweets and confectionary. They had bought a fleet of six more vehicles to help with the expansion. In doing so, however, the business was left badly in debt, eventually owing more that £10,000 and leaving the Richards in desperate need of capital. The family business including confectionary may have explained Clive's interest in sweet shops when committing his crimes.

Clive lived in a 'Walter Mitty' world and told interviewing officers that as a child he had been abducted by a group of people because he was so intelligent. He had been selected along with children from America, Germany, Holland and France and they had all been kept in an underground bunker to be experimented on. It was during one of these experiments that an accident had occurred and he had been exposed to certain gases that resulted in him becoming overweight ever since. His parents obviously knew nothing of this and simply described him as a lad with an imagination. Clive's fabricated story of his childhood abduction was very detailed, he was able to name the other children abducted and claimed to have some documents at home bearing their details. It was obvious that these fantasies were not something that he had created following the murder but stories he had developed over many years.

When searching his bedroom there were lots of letters allegedly from his foreign friends but none of these appeared to have been sent from abroad. They were all written in a type of hieroglyphics that only he could understand.

An expert in the field of writing could not make any sense of the letters and concluded they were total gibberish. Richards stated that he had kept in regular contact with his foreign childhood genius friends, but although he could supply names, he was unable to supply any further details to track them down or explain how he kept in contact with them. Enquiries by INTERPOL failed to identify or locate any of the named people and it was concluded that they did not exist.

Newspaper report following arrest and charge of Clive Richards – Bristol Evening Post May 1986

Richards claimed that he was a professor of Nonetics and Totetology, employed by the Department of Environment doing a top-secret conservation study. He explained that he had spent time in London surveying the homeless population and was visiting Portsmouth to continue his studies on the day he was arrested there. It was due to working within the homeless environment that he felt the need to arm himself with a knife and iron bar for self-protection. The Department of Environment had no knowledge of Clive Richards and it was established that the words Nonetics and Totetology did not exist, there was no such science for him to be a professor of. They were yet again complete figments of Richards' imagination.

Richards was charged with the murder of Roy Page and remanded in custody awaiting trial.

Clive Richards entered a not guilty plea at his trial for the murder of Roy Page in April 1986 and listened attentively to the numerous witnesses called throughout the eight-day trial. Various witnesses who had seen him in Bristol that day, and subsequently identified him from identity parades, were called and gave evidence for the prosecution as to what they had seen. The investigating officers gave evidence as to the circumstances of Richards' arrest and how they were able to place him at the scene of the crime. Scribbling furiously on a notebook he had by his side, Richards at times shook his head in denial or disbelief whilst witnesses were giving evidence. A psychiatrist from Broadmoor Secure Hospital gave evidence that Richards' fantasies for working in the field of 'Nonetics' were the result of a mental illness. Dr Harvey Gordon had examined Richards during his time on remand and said of Richards: *"On balance, I think he is suffering from severe mental illness, normally known as chronic schizophrenia."*

I was present throughout the trial of Clive Richards and at no time did he ever change the story that he had given in interview. He had grown to believe it himself and was suffering from mental health problems. The psychiatrists however were satisfied that he had no defence open to him due to his mental illness, describing him as highly intelligent but strange. They felt he would have known what he was doing at the time of the murder and was responsible for his actions. The defence were unable to locate or call any of the super intelligent foreign friends that Richards had spoken about in interview to support his assertions. Clive Richards was still insistent that he had never visited Bristol other than in 1970 when the SS Great Britain had returned to Bristol docks for restoration.

With regards to the fingerprint evidence that placed Clive Richards in Bristol at the time of the murder, his defence barrister Charles Barton tried to argue that the fingerprint evidence should be excluded.

Mr Barton's reasoning was based around the standard requirement for a fingerprint expert to identify 15 matching characteristics between a suspect's fingerprints and an impression found at a crime scene. He argued that each partial print only had ten characteristics that matched, so each one alone was not good enough to make an identification so should not be allowed. If looked at independently, each should be excluded as not good enough.

The fingerprint expert pointed out that the very same standards referred to by Mr Barton, also directed that two impressions found on one exhibit, only required 10 matching characteristics each, as they did in this case. The expert was satisfied that the prints were those of Clive Richards and the identification was in line with the standards set.

Clive Richards stood in the witness box to give evidence. He spoke articulately and claimed he was not guilty throughout, but each time he was presented with evidence that contradicted this claim, he launched into stories that were so complex and bizarre that they became impossible to believe and too complex to follow. At points throughout the proceedings, it became difficult to accept that the man in the dock was nothing more than a fantasist and placed doubt on whether he was capable of being a brutal killer. This was possibly what the defense were hoping to portray to convince the jury that Richards was not guilty of murder.

The prosecuting barristers summed up the evidence and told the jury that they could be satisfied that Clive Richards was guilty of the murder of Roy Page. Mr Barton claimed that his client was not guilty, and that the fingerprint evidence should be ignored. He also suggested that if the jury accepted the fingerprint evidence, they should still find him not guilty on the grounds of mental illness.

After only 6 hours of jury deliberation, Richards was found guilty of murder and sentenced to life imprisonment. He has never accepted that he was responsible for the murder and continues writing to himself in hieroglyphics.

Following the verdict, the Judge, Justice Rose said:

"You are a clever, arrogant, and dangerous man. Had it not been for the observation and prompt action of a number of inhabitants of Portsmouth, I fear you would have committed other very grave offences which you had already planned."

Richards was then taken down to start his life sentence. After his sentencing, Lew Clark said:

"I quite agree with the judge's remarks. Think of the way he was armed when he was arrested. He had a heavy iron bar and a sheath knife in his bag – why did he have that lot? I haven't any doubt myself that he was out to commit robbery at least that day. And if opposed, he would have used as much violence as necessary to achieve his ends. That's my opinion. That will always be my opinion."

There is no doubt that, without the assistance of Crimewatch UK, this crime would never have been detected. It was also Clive Richard's downfall that he hadn't watched the programme on that night.

As was normal practice in the 1980's, after every successful murder investigation, officers engaged in the investigation were presented with a tie to mark the occasion. A Crimewatch themed tie was created depicting a book with page 158 missing representing the

fact that Mr Page lived at 158 St John's Lane. I
am still the proud owner of mine.

The Murder of Jenny King 1998

Chapter 1:

The Crime

By 1998, I had been promoted to the rank of sergeant and for the past 7 years had held the rank of Detective Sergeant. I was now working in the Staplehill CID office along with two other sergeants and 24 detectives. There was an average of 10 murders a year in the Avon and Somerset area although the figures were slowly increasing. Whenever a murder occurs, the hosting district requests staff from neighbouring districts to support the enquiry. I was often one of the first to offer my services, and because of the experience I had amassed over the years, I was normally tasked with one of the key roles within the incident room. These roles being:

Receiver: They get to view all information first as it arrives in an incident room and decide what urgent initial action is required.

Document Reader: They have to read all documentation in great detail to decide if all lines of investigation have been followed and to decide how documents should be recorded within the HOLMES computer system ensuring any links with other evidence are recognised.

Action Allocator: They allocate all the work to the detectives to ensure work is evenly distributed but also that action teams work on specific themes to avoid any duplication.

My favourite role was the Receiver although this was often the most pressurised position to hold. The pressure came from the sheer quantity of material generated in an investigation of this nature. There is a need to keep on top of the 'In tray' to ensure that important evidence is not missed or left sitting unactioned in the in tray for long periods. Delaying in actioning work can mean important evidence is lost.

It was a cold wet winter's evening, in fact it was the night before Halloween and as it was a Friday, it seemed as though most of Bristol's youth were out drinking and dancing the night away. Jenny King was among this group. She was 22 years old, slim build with long straight dark hair that came halfway down her back. She was employed as a secretary/receptionist by a local business in Warmley and loved her job.

Jenny was very popular with her friends as she was full of fun and great to be with. On that evening, Jenny had gone out wearing black bootleg trousers, black platform shoes, a sparkly black sleeveless top and her brother's black leather jacket. Jenny had a boyfriend called Steven Daly but this was still quite a new relationship. Steven was 30 and worked for a soft drinks firm in Longwell Green, near Bristol, they were both happy and had decided to have separate evenings out with their own group of friends.

Jenny still lived at home with her parents Ray and Margaret as well as her 25-year-old brother Andrew and 13-year-old sister Sarah. Ray and Margaret were away on holiday in Tenby that weekend with Sarah, so Jenny and Andrew had the house to themselves. Ray and Margaret had agreed that Steven could stay in the house overnight with Jenny whilst they were away.

Jenny headed off to the centre of Bristol with her close friend Claire, they travelled together by bus because they were both intending to drink and to have an enjoyable time without the concerns of driving home at the end of the evening. The two of them visited various pubs such as 'The Slug and Lettuce', 'Edwards' and 'Yates Wine Bar'. They had met several friends during the night but had remained together. At 11:10pm, Jenny and Claire parted company, Jenny wished to go on to a nightclub until the early hours and this did not suit Claire. Jenny explained that she was going to catch a bus up to Kingswood and then finish the evening at 'Chasers' nightclub. That was to be the last times that Claire saw Jenny.

Jenny King and boyfriend Steven Daly

Chasers Club

Jenny arrived at 'Chasers' club situated on High Street in the Kingswood area of Bristol, she was alone as she entered the club at about 11:35pm, but she soon met many people she knew inside the club. In fact, Jenny's brother Andrew was also at 'Chasers' and they spoke several times during the night.   A friend of

Jenny's, Georgina can recall talking to her in the club and she found her to be in good spirits, planning a day trip for her 13-year-old sister in the days to come. She recalled Jenny being very merry but not too drunk that she was slurring her words or unsteady on her feet. Whilst talking to her, Georgina recalled Jenny looking across the dance floor and saying:

"There goes my ex-psycho boyfriend."

Georgina looked across the room but could not see anyone specific and did not know who Jenny was referring to.

At 1:30am, Andrew bought his sister a drink and enquired how she was intending to get home. He gave her £5 to get a taxi, as she had mentioned that she had spent all her money on drinks and food and only had a little loose change left so was intending to walk the mile home.

Jenny collected her brother's jacket and walked out of Chasers alone and headed towards Kingswood High Street. The CCTV camera outside captured her departure, showing Jenny leaving the nightclub alone at 2:10am.

Jenny had invited her boyfriend Steven to stay with her that weekend so was eager to get home and see him.

Taxis normally park up in a taxi rank on Kingswood High Street awaiting the club goers to head home but Jenny made the decision to walk. She had walked this route home on many occasions and knew it would only take her about 20 minutes. She headed left along High Street and into Hill Street continuing on towards her home in Warmley.

The next part of the story is my interpretation of what is likely to have happened as Jenny's murderer has never chosen to give his true account of events. I have based my account on the evidence later gathered during the investigation, added some details about the suspect's demeanour having learnt the type of person he was. Feel free to put your own slant on the case as it is only Jenny and her attacker who know the truth.

I believe that she saw the lad approaching her, slowly catching her up as she was about half way down Hill Street, I imagine things continued something like this:

He called out *"Hey don't I know you?"* or words to that effect. (It is quite possible that he knew Jenny by sight as his grandparents lived close to Jenny's house).

She turned around to face him to see a smartly dressed young man. His face looking familiar but she could not put a name to him.

He said. *"You must be cold. Are you sure you don't need someone to put their arms around you."*

Jenny was used to men trying to chat her up, she wasn't frightenend and simply ignored his advances and continued to walk ahead in a confident manner. He offered to accompany her as he was walking in the same direction anyway. Jenny was polite and friendly but was not interested in having company as she was only ten minutes from home and was quite happy to be alone, knowing her boyfriend would be waiting for her.

As she reached Tennis Court Road, she told the man that she knew of a short cut back to where she lived and suggested that they part company and go their own way. He continued to walk alongside her, and no doubt liked the fact that he was making her feel a little uncomfortable, this possibly even excited him. Jenny's short cut took her alongside a small copse and as they walked past this wooded area, the man grabbed Jenny around the neck and waist and dragged her into the centre of the copse.

He told her not to shout out if she didn't want to get hurt. He told Jenny to remove her trousers and knickers so, in fear for her safety, she started to undo the trousers and lower them to the ground. He was getting impatient and told her to hurry up, pushing her to the ground. Jenny fought back and started to scream. Her knickers had by this point been removed and to keep her quiet, he punched her several times in the face and wrapped the trousers which had her knickers caught up in them around her neck in the form of a ligature and started to pull them tightly.

The screams began to fade as Jenny lost consciousness and was strangled to death.

Jenny had put up quite a fight and the man was now in a panic. He was annoyed at Jenny for not submitting to his demands, so he picked up a tree branch and used it to sexually assault her. He then stood up, it was pitch black and he could see very little around him. He fumbled to find the one and only pathway into and out of the copse, and accidently stood on Jenny's lifeless body on the ground. Finally locating the pathway, he exited the copse, and walked quickly home, calming his rapid breathing with each step he took.

The man arrived home at about 3:30am on the morning of the murder. When he searched for his house keys, he could not find them; he knew he had locked up when he left for his night out in town, so he must have lost the keys at some point during the evening. There was nothing he could do other than bang on the back door and wake up his mother. He was otherwise quite calm and when his mother let him in, he showed no signs of any panic. He said good night and went to bed, sleeping without a second thought for Jenny.

Steven Daly arrived at Jenny's house at about 2:15am and had to let himself in by means of a concealed key. When Steven woke the following morning and realised that Jenny was still not home, he started to get a little concerned. He had to go to work that day because he was a delivery driver, and the customers were reliant upon the goods being supplied. He phoned Jenny's home four or five times during the day but got no reply. As soon as he finished work, he drove straight back to

Jenny's house but there was no sign of Jenny. He contacted Andrew so that the two of them could phone around all of Jenny's friends in case she had stayed with one of them. This was not like Jenny; she was so reliable and would always phone home to stop anyone worrying about her. It was so out of character for Jenny not to let the family know so Andrew called his parents to get their views on what he should do. Ray and Margaret knew something was seriously wrong and called short their break and headed home. They instructed Andrew to phone the police to report Jenny missing.

At 7pm on Saturday the 31st of October 1998, Jenny King was reported as a missing person to the police at Staple Hill.

I reported for duty as normal at Staple Hill CID at 8:00am on that Sunday the 1st of November, I was the Detective Sergeant covering the weekend duties with reduced staffing levels which was normal for the weekend. The uniform Inspector popped into my office and handed me a missing person report that was giving him some concern. Normally missing people are dealt with by the uniform department for the first few days as that is the period when most missing people turn up. The standard missing person investigation involves an ongoing log being maintained of enquiries made and the duty uniform inspector overseeing matters. This was not a vulnerable missing person, there were no concerns about Jenny being depressed so no real reason for the uniform inspector to retain the enquiries. This case was different, something felt wrong and after talking to the family, it was apparent that it was so out of character for Jenny to disappear in this way that it was believed that she may have come to some harm. For a 22-year-old to be reported as a missing person, without any background of vulnerability, it was not uncommon for a very limited investigation to be carried out until 24 hours had passed. I decided that I too was concerned and that the CID should immediately take over the enquiries.

I could sense that this was not a normal missing person situation and immediately commenced a crime investigation, raising individual actions for officers to conduct. It was by taking this step that no time was lost and evidence such as CCTV was gathered immediately. Creating actions rather than using an ongoing log would also assist in the future should the investigation be transferred onto the HOLMES computer system.

I contacted Detective Chief Inspector Geoff Anderson at home as he was the senior detective on the district. He agreed with my assessment of the case and stated that he would give a press statement that day describing Jenny and asking for anyone who could assist with any sightings of her from the moment she left 'Chasers'.

Detective Constables Ashwin and Pesticcio were given the onerous task of being family liaison officers. They would keep in regular contact with the entire King family and be there to provide support throughout, whatever the outcome of the investigation. This is a very stressful role within a major enquiry, often having to deal with very emotional situations and becoming close to the grieving family.

I started by taking the initial control of the investigation until senior officers were identified to lead the enquiry. All family and friends were contacted to trace Jenny. The video tapes of 'Chasers' and all local premises were seized. Andrew was eventually able to identify his sister on the CCTV entering and leaving 'Chasers' which gave the investigation team a starting a point.

Enquiries were made at all the local hospitals and all the local taxi companies but no useful information was gleaned.

Having spoken to Georgina, it was necessary to identify 'the ex-psycho boyfriend' that Jenny had referred to inside the club. Any ex-boyfriends would need to be identified and traced.

The family liaison officers had to speak with the family about any previous relationships their daughter had. They also needed to seize Jenny's hairbrush in case the DNA from her hair was the only way the police could identify a body should she be found dead in months or years to come. It was decided that the investigation should be carried out using the Home Office Linked Major Enquiry System (HOLMES). This is a computer system for recording indexing and collating all information gathered and is a system that I was well experienced in using.

The size of the enquiry team had already by day 2 increased to 30 officers and Detective Superintendent Bill Davies was the nominated Senior Investigating Officer. I had been given my favourite role of 'Receiver', which meant that any information received in the incident room would come to me first. Little did I know at the start just how much information would come into the enquiry.

There was a well-established system of having three 'In Trays' coloured green, yellow or red to indicate the priority of the document. This system was not able to cope with the volume of paperwork generated and soon three coloured crates instead of trays had to be used and these were full to overflowing.

Extensive searches were carried out along the route Jenny was believed to have walked towards home and the police helicopter was used to search for heat spots in overgrown areas of land. I had the opportunity to go up in the helicopter to direct the officers to the areas of greatest interest. The search continued over the next few days by trained search teams.

The first press release had pointed out the possibility that Jenny had taken a taxi from the nightclub. Andrew had given her money for a taxi so at that point there was no reason to believe that she had not taken a taxi. We were considering the possibility that a bogus taxi could have been involved or that she had shared a taxi. A photograph of Jenny was released asking the public if they had seen her on the night of her disappearance or since.

*The photograph of Jenny
circulated to the public*

The public response was more than we could have imagined. We received reports of taxi drivers who had behaved inappropriately in the past, possible bogus taxis because the drivers had not known the fare. We became inundated with information from the public trying to assist. Hundreds of calls came into the incident room about taxi drivers alone.

The media was only one aspect of our investigation but this generated a mass of work. There was national interest because Jenny was a pretty 22-year-old female who had disappeared on her way home from a night club. The public reported hearing screams on the night of the murder in all areas of Bristol. The fact that it had been Halloween made it difficult to prove if any scream could have been linked to the attack on Jenny. There were reported sightings of Jenny all over the country, as well as Ireland and France. My Receiver 'In Tray' was added to by 1000 new documents each day.

As is often the case in high profile police investigations, there was a fair share of psychics and dowsers predicting where Jenny would be found and who was responsible for her disappearance? We could not ignore these predictions, but they were placed well down on our priority list. None of these people got anywhere near the truth.

A reconstruction of Jenny's last known movements was shown on television. A female officer played the role of Jenny and she slowly walked the route Jenny was by that time believed to have taken. We had fairly well ruled out the idea that Jenny had taken a taxi. This reconstruction resulted in a member of the public coming forward reporting that she had seen Jenny halfway down Hill Street talking to an unknown male at about 2am. She made a statement and identified Jenny from a group of images of females of a similar general description. Was this the offender speaking with the victim?

*Roy and Margaret King
at press conference*

*Police officer
participating in
reconstruction*

The enquiries into Jenny's ex-boyfriends had revealed one person that sparked an interest. It was a young man called Mark Stone who had gone out with Jenny for about six months in 1995. Jenny had ended the relationship as she felt Mark was getting too serious. Mark took things badly and took a long time to accept the relationship had finished. We decided to look into Mark's background in detail, as he was a person that had been besotted by Jenny, could he be her 'Psycho ex-boyfriend?' Enquiries were made with Mark's current girlfriend who provided him with a partial alibi for the night of the murder, but he could not be fully alibied. He denied having been in Chasers club on the night of the murder, which if true meant we had still not identified the 'psycho ex-boyfriend'.

Bill Davies decided that he wished to identify all 450 people who attended Chasers night club on the Halloween night celebrations in case the offender had followed Jenny from the club. A team headed by Detective Sergeant Derek Barnet, was given this task occupying a large room at Kingswood police station. Photographic stills were taken from the clubs CCTV, each was numbered and pinned on boards in the viewing room. The public were invited to view the stills and slowly but surely names were marked against the faces. The team successfully identified 320 people but Mark Stone was not among this group and no obvious offender was identified.

Jenny's friends informed the police of another male, Ralph Flay who had a fixation on her. He lived in Hill Street on the route that Jenny would have taken to walk home. He had been following and pestering her for several months, giving her unwanted flowers on a couple of occasions. Ralph suffered from mental health issues and had some learning difficulties, he used to refer to Jenny as his girlfriend although this was clearly not the case. Ralph's parents believed he was at home on the night of the murder but as they were asleep, he could not be fully alibied. Jenny's friends had described him as strange so was this the person Jenny had referred to as being in Chasers? Ralph was not found on any of the photographs from Chasers CCTV.

The investigation and search team had now reached 200 officers and they were all working long hours to locate Jenny. She was still a missing person but there was little doubt that she had come to harm.

Having worked all through Sunday night and into Monday, I was at last due to head home to catch up on lost sleep. There was still no news of Jenny. As I drove home from Kingswood police station, I took the route Jenny would have walked or gone by car if she had been driven. I could not help noticing two wooded areas that I felt were the most likely place for Jenny to have been attacked or to have collapsed in a drunken stupor. I was so drawn to these wooded areas that I parked up on the roundabout at the bottom of Hill Street at the junction with the ring road and stared into the wooded area. Little did I know at the time that I was not too far away from where she would eventually be found. Time was getting on and she had to be found soon, we already knew it was highly unlikely to find her alive but we had to keep our hopes up.

Support Group are a team of specialist search officers, they organised the searches that needed to be conducted. Systematic searches continued, under the guidance of experts who suggested that the area nearest 'Chasers' was the most likely place for Jenny to be found. Those officers leading the investigation were less convinced and with their knowledge of the vicinity and route home that Jenny would have taken, they suggested searches be concentrated around the two wooded areas near Firework Close.

At 2:30pm on Tuesday the 3rd of November 1998, Police Constable 592 Mark Thompson entered a small, wooded copse at Firework Close and discovered Jenny's semi-naked body lying on her back. The officer's training instantly kicked in and he carefully retraced his steps to the entrance of the copse ensuring that he did not disturb any potential evidence. He reported his find to the rest of the search team and they protected the scene until others arrived.

The feelings within the incident room were mixed. Jenny was dead so everyone was devastated. The only good thing about finding her body was that, at last, the family could start their grieving and would have a body to bury. There have been cases in the past where no body has ever been discovered and the family had been left always wondering. The other advantage about having found Jenny was that the Forensic experts would now have a chance of gathering evidence against any future suspects.

The section of copse where Jenny had been found was known locally as the den. Local children would often enter the den for a secret smoke. There was only really one entry/exit to the den so that had to be the way that the murderer had gone in and out. To reduce any possibility that the scene of crime and forensic teams would destroy any evidence, it was decided to cut a separate path through the trees into the den. The support group officers spent hours with cutting equipment such as hedge trimmers, scythes and axes creating a new entry path.

The Pathologist, Forensic Scientist and Scene of Crime Officers could then carry out their examination of the scene without anything having been disturbed first. You often see on the television that square metal plates are placed on the ground to protect evidence but with the soft earth in the den these were considered as unsuitable.

Jenny was lying on her back and was naked from the waist down. Her black sparkly top was pulled up exposing her bra and the leather jacket was partly down over her shoulders as if restricting the movement of her arms. Jenny's trousers and knickers had been removed and were tightly tied around her neck with the ends pushed into her mouth. Jenny had a large bruise to her left eye and cheek, so she had received quite a substantial blow to the face. She also had numerous scratches on her body which were consistent with having been scratched by the brambles in the den. It looked like Jenny had put up quite a fight and had to be prevented from shouting out.

The Forensic Scientist, Clair Galbraith took several tapings from the body which was simply a matter of dabbing large strips of sticky tape over the body to collect any fibres or foreign material that were present. The strips were each marked to show where on the body or clothing they had been applied as this could be vital to know later in examinations back at the laboratory. It was during this process that a faint mark in mud was discovered on Jenny's exposed abdomen. This was photographed and would become an important piece of evidence in the case. Samples of soil from the den and surrounding area were taken for any future analysis if relevant. Once this had been done, Jenny's body was removed from the scene for a post-mortem examination.

On the evening of the 3rd of November, Home Office Pathologist Dr Hugh White conducted a post-mortem and concluded that the cause of death was strangulation by means of the ligature around her neck. The muddy marks on Jenny's body were examined more closely and although not clear, a faint shoe impression could be seen. Hugh White also found a pubic hair, which appeared different than Jenny's other pubic hair. This was carefully bagged up for submission to the forensic science laboratory at Chepstow. There were no items from the scene that were likely to reveal fingerprint evidence although attempts were made to fingerprint the victims clothing.

A fingertip search of the den area which lasted two days revealed the usual assortment of items such as cigarette ends, chewing gum, bottles, crisp bags, knives, used condoms and all of these proved to have nothing to do with this case. The significant finds were: 38 pence in loose change found 3" from the deceased's feet and two keys on separate key rings but joined together found at the same location.

The keys showed no sign of damage, rusting or weathering so the find was considered significant and possibly the keys of an offender as they did not belong to Jenny. The keys were assigned the exhibit numbers 8199AJR55A & 8199AJR55B.

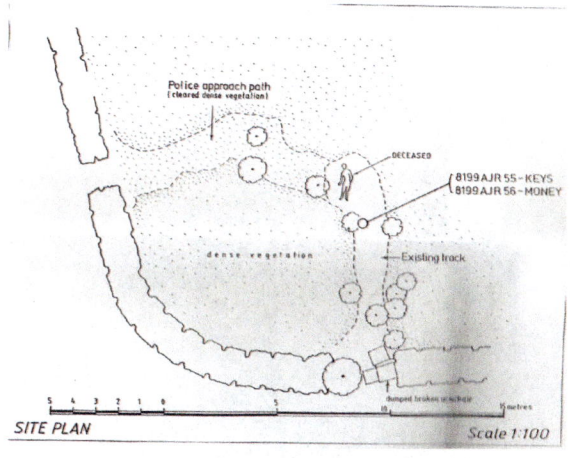

The Copse

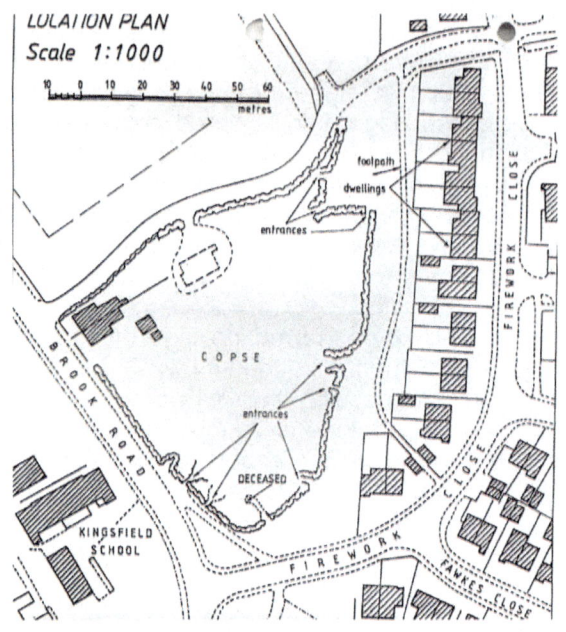

Deposition Site

Selection of rubbish found in the den

Police Constables Ashwin and Pesticcio had the job of notifying the King family that the body of a young female had been found about 200 yards from their home and that the description of the woman and clothing did fit that of Jenny.

As soon as Mr King identified his daughter's body, there was a new press release. Mr and Mrs King made a personal plea for anyone with information to come forward. Due to the scratches on Jenny, it was suggested that the offender could also have been injured during the attack.

This mention in the media alone led to several hundred calls into the incident room naming individuals with cuts and scratches that could be the offender. Some sightings were reported of people as far away as Leicester bearing scratches. My in tray once again overflowed with documents.

It was a mammoth task, particularly for me, dealing first with all material coming into the room. We were under a great deal of pressure to catch the murderer and to catch him quickly. We now believed that we had the murderer's keys. A policy decision was made by Bill Davies that whenever any strong suspect was identified, the keys would be tried out in their house locks as part of the elimination process. The fact that keys had been found was not released to the public. It is quite normal to hold back certain evidence or information as this can be used to test any admissions by people claiming to be the offender.

On the 9th of November, it was decided to carry out a covert operation during the hours of darkness and to try out copies of the recovered keys in selected locks. This was to include Steven Daly's home, the home address of the ex-boyfriend Mark Stone and the home of Ralph Flay.

Bill Davies kept this tactic very quiet and only told a few people who needed to know. I was asked if I would work throughout the night to provide continuity for the keys. I had to sign out the keys to officers from the Force Targeting team and collect them in the morning. I took the opportunity to work quietly alone without the phone to disturb me. I had the whole night to work through my three 'In Trays' and by the morning they were all empty. The documents having been assessed by me, necessary actions raised and documents moved along the incident room chain to be indexed, typed and read. It felt nice to know that I was at last on top of the paperwork and nothing important was hidden amongst documents in the crates. Unfortunately, once I returned to work the next day the trays were close to filling up again.

The covert team waited until about 2am until they approached Mr Stone's front door. The first key they tried entered the lock and with a slight bit of jiggling, operated the lock and opened the front door. What a stroke of luck! After consultation with Superintendent Davies, they then knocked at the door and arrested Mark

Stone for the murder of Jenny King. He was taken to Staplehill police station and his home address was searched. Mark was examined by a police surgeon and found to have numerous small cuts to his hands which appeared several days old. Seized from his house were all his shoes, clothes in particular green coloured clothing and door locks. It was obvious, by speaking with his partner, that Mark was a very possessive intense person.

In interview, Stone stated he had not seen Jenny King in years and was not responsible for her murder. He stated that he was at home with his partner at the time of the attack and she confirmed it.

Due to the need for an urgent opinion, a local locksmith examined Stone's front door lock and the keys recovered from the scene and made a statement stating he was 99 per cent sure that one of the keys was made for the front door lock. We could not find a second lock connected with Stone that could account for the second key recovered. Stone denied he had ever lost any keys. The locksmith's views on the surface appeared strong evidence.

The injuries to Stone's hands had occurred at work and were in fact reported at the time to the medical officer. His alibi was confirmed with his girlfriend and the entry in his works record of injury book, dated 26.10.98 accounted for his scratches.

Senior Officers at police HQ were pushing for Stone to be charged with Jenny's murder but Bill was not happy. The interviewing officers were telling him that they were convinced that Stone was innocent. Bill made the decision to trust his interviewing officers' instincts and released Mark Stone on bail to carryout additional tests.

The evidence against Stone was reliant on a local locksmith and this needed to be tested further. A forensic locksmith, Mr Crummack, from London was asked to examine the lock seized from Stone's front door and the keys 8199AJR55A & B found at the murder scene. He was satisfied that they were not a match. He was able to show that Mark Stone's front door lock was a very cheap front door lock and very worn. The lock specification, although quite close to that of the recovered key, was slightly different and this had meant that the lock and key did not match but the key had picked the worn lock when it appeared to fit. The decision not to charge Stone had been the correct one.

The covert operation did not halt, officers were tasked with trying the keys at Ralph Flay's home address in Hill Street. In the early hours of one morning, they crept up to the front door, inserted the key and as they did so the door swung open. Flay was arrested and his front door lock was seized. He denied all knowledge of the offence. Mr Crummack's services were again used, this time he examined Flay's door lock and the keys 8199AJR55A & B. He described the lock fitted to Flay's front door as like a hotel room door lock. The door had never in fact been locked at the time the officers had tested the keys. The process of turning the key in the lock had made the whole handle turn and the door open. The same would have happened had a screwdriver been inserted into the lock. He concluded that the key was once again not the correct configuration for the lock. Flay was released on bail.

The Forensic scientists were busy checking all the items submitted to them. Clair Galbraith being the lead scientist had examined all the tapings from Jenny's body and all of Jenny's clothing and she had found several green polyester and cotton fibres that could not be accounted for as well as the pubic hair which did not microscopically match those of Jenny. The term not a microscopic match simply means that the pubic hair did not look similar under a microscope and this was mainly due to colour differences.

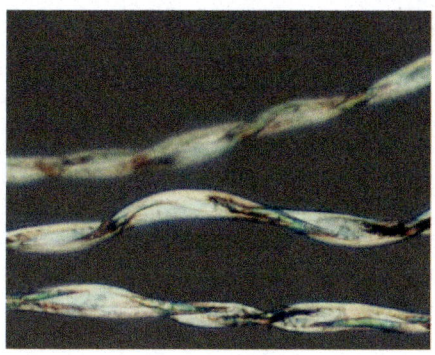

Microscopic green cotton fibres

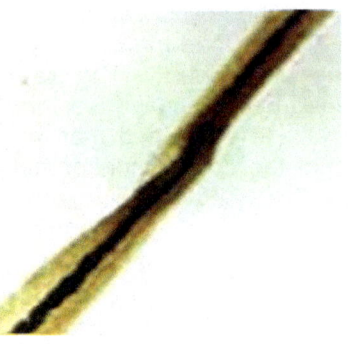

Microscopic human pubic hair

Because the leather jacket worn by Jenny had belonged to her brother Andrew, we had to recover any green shirts that he owned to submit them to the laboratory to see if they could have been the source of the fibre. None of the 5 shirts proved to be the source of the green fibres.

Scientist Mr Ian Steel-Gray examined the muddy foot impression found on Jenny's abdomen and was able to give some idea of the tread pattern of the shoes that had made the mark. It was not a common pattern and the national records of shoe marks were not able to come up with a common make of shoe with the relevant tread pattern.

The senior investigators Bill Davies and Geoff Anderson had not initially wished to release to the press the fact that keys had been found at the murder scene as this was one piece of evidence, they believed could trap the offender. As time went on however, it was decided to ask the public for assistance in identifying the keys.

Detective Superintendent Bill Davies showing keys to the public

Close up of recovered keys

Against the advice of Headquarters CID, Detective Superintendent Davies decided to release to the public, the fact that two keys had been found near to where Jenny had been found. A photograph of these two keys was plastered all over the newspapers and hundreds of calls started to come in suggesting the types of locks that the keys would operate as well as reporting people changing their locks.

Chapter 2:

The Break

The break came on the 10th of November as a direct result of the press release regarding the keys. Three calls were received during the 10th and 11th November from Mr Jennings. He reported the fact that on the night that Jenny disappeared, his nephew Paul Hunt had lost his house keys when he was out and about in Bristol, and they looked similar to the keys found at the scene. He went on to explain that Paul Hunt had walked home through Kingswood and Warmley, which were not too far from the scene of the murder. Mr Jennings had asked Paul to report the loss to the police, but Paul had declined so that was why Mr Jennings had made the phone call himself. Paul Hunt did in fact call the police after Mr Jennings insisted because he knew his uncle had reported the loss. Mr Jennings did not suspect for a moment that his nephew was responsible for the murder but he felt that the police needed to know about the keys.

At 11:35am on the 11th of November, officers were sent to Paul Hunt's home address in Malvern Drive, Cadbury Heath, Bristol where they were greeted by Paul and his mother. The officers explained why they were there and requested permission to test the keys in the house locks. The recovered keys fitted both the front and rear doors to the premises. The officers then arrested Paul Hunt for the murder of Jenny King. The locks were seized RM1(Rear door lock) and RM2 (Front door lock). We arranged for brand new replacement locks to be fitted to keep the house secure.

Euro Profile

Door lock and key of type recovered

We also seized from the home address all the spare sets of keys that the family had for the two locks. There were three sets for the front door exhibited as IH1, TSA2 and 1313MFP03. There was one spare key for the rear door exhibited as TSA1. We were told that this accounted for all the spare keys.

Hunt was taken to Staplehill police station for interview by a team of trained interviewing officers.

Paul Hunt was a 22-year-old lad who lived in the Cadbury Heath area of Bristol about 2 miles from Jenny's home. He lived with his mother; he was an only child whose father left home when he was five. He had in fact attended the same primary school as Jenny, but they were in a year apart and it is not known if they ever knew each other to speak to. In 1985 due to his disruptive behaviour involving violence towards other pupils he was excluded from school.

In December of 1985 Paul Hunt was involved in a car accident and suffered severe injuries requiring him to be hospitalised.

Paul was cautioned in 1992 for making indecent phone calls to a fellow school pupil at St Bernard Lovell school and it was alleged that he indecently assaulted a girl at the same school. He was cautioned in 1993 for two offences of indecent exposure when on separate occasions, he masturbated in front of females whilst a passenger on a train. Intelligence checks revealed that he had been caught having stolen ladies' underwear from a washing line a few streets from his home address about two years earlier and was given a verbal warning. Paul, you will read later, had become obsessed with making threatening or abusive calls in the months prior to the murder.

People that knew Paul described him as a quiet person, hard worker and friendly. He had a steady girlfriend and was like any other boy next door. Paul was a factory worker at Creda in Yate.

When the Hunt's home address was searched, a green 'Ralph Lauren' shirt 1313MFP29 was found and seized along with two other green shirts. Officers also found a pair of 'Truka' make shoes which appeared to have a similar tread pattern to that described by Mr Steel-Gray.

Green Ralph Lauren shirt

Truka shoes

Paul's mother was quick to point out that the 'Truka' shoes could have nothing to do with the crime as they were in fact a pair she acquired on the 2nd of November, two days after the offence. She went on to explain that Paul had owned a previous pair of 'Truka' shoes, but they hurt his feet and were taken back to the shop under complaint on the 2nd of November, and the pair being seized was a pair Paul was given as a replacement. The shop in question was Mastershoe in Bond Street, Bristol.

Paul's mother explained that it was the shoes she had returned to Mastershoe that were the pair of shoes that Paul was wearing on the night of Jenny's murder. Although 9 days had passed since the shoes had been returned to the shop, we immediately sent a team to Mastershoe. They successfully recovered what they believed to be Paul Hunt's returned shoes that he had been wearing on the night of 30th/31st October 1998.

There were several shoes in the returns box at the shop but only one pair of 'Truka' shoes. The manager explained that they tended to empty the returns box as soon as it filled up, roughly every week but the only reason it had not been cleared was the fact that not many shoes had been returned under complaint. With the help of records and differing styles of shoes, it was easy to identify the correct ones. The store manager told us that had we left it two days longer before making these enquiries with Mastershoe, the returns would all have been sent back to the distributors and destroyed. Paperwork in the shop confirmed Paul Hunt's mother had returned them on the date she claimed.

Paul Hunt was examined by a police surgeon whilst in custody and was found to have numerous long scratches on his body with the most significant being 6" long on his buttocks. He was later to suggest that these were caused whilst sitting on waste metal bins at work. Paul stated that most of the metal workers received minor injuries on a regular basis.

A sample of Paul Hunt's pubic hair was also taken for submission to the laboratory.

Paul Hunt

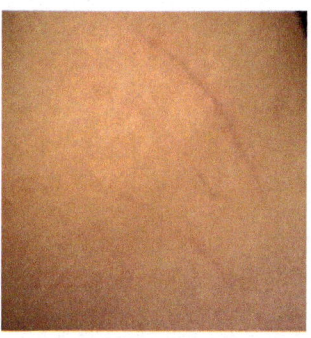

Hunt's body scratches

The forensic experts now set about their work. Clair Galbraith carried out initial checks on the green 'Ralph Lauren' shirt 1313MFP29 and found the fibres to be a microscopic match to the fibres found on Jenny's body.

Clair pursued the examination of the green fibres further and was able to state that, not only the microscopic appearance of the fibres matched Hunt's Ralph Lauren shirt but also the chemical composition of the dyes in the fibres found on Jenny's body were the same as those that made up Paul Hunt's 'Ralph Lauren' shirt. This was good supporting evidence that Paul had been in contact with Jenny at some point. Consideration was given to trying to find out how many green 'Ralph Lauren' shirts of that precise colour were imported into the country, but that avenue was not pursued once we had recovered and viewed a videotape of Paul Hunt leaving McCluskeys nightclub in the early hours of Saturday the 31st of October. This clearly showed Hunt wearing his green 'Ralph Lauren' shirt on the night of the murder. This evidence fitted well with the evidence Clair Galbraith had found.

Mr Steel-Gray found that the shoe pattern in mud left on Jenny's body was similar to that of the shoes recovered from Mastershoe. The tread of the recovered shoes was found to have a quantity of soil within them. This was carefully removed and was sent off to a renowned sedimentologist, Professor Pye in Reading to compare this soil with the samples taken from the den where Jenny had been found.

Ian Steel-Gray in the meantime was experimenting with the footmark on Jenny's body. Using different light sources he was able to make the images clearer. He had a stroke of luck because the tread pattern on Paul Hunt's 'Truka' shoes was very rare. Mr Steel-Gray was able to say that the mark on the body was made by a similar tread pattern and it had to be from a shoe of size 9 or 10. Paul Hunt wore size 9. Ian Steel-Gray was also able to compare the wear pattern on the mark. When shoes are worn, the tread slowly wears away unevenly, and this differs from one person's shoes to another as we all walk and apply pressure to our soles in different ways. He was able to say that the amount of wear and the areas worn on the mark left on the body were identical to that on Paul Hunt's shoes and this provided further strong support that Paul Hunt had trodden on Jenny. Just in case Hunt should suggest that the shoes recovered from Mastershoe were the wrong pair, further tests were carried out to compare the wear inside the shoes where toes rub on the leather. These shoes were compared with other pairs of Hunt's shoes recovered from his home and there were numerous similarities of areas where Hunt's toes had marked the leather uppers on his shoes. This was conclusive proof that the shoes Mrs Hunt stated were worn by Paul on the night of the murder and that had been recovered from Mastershoe, were Paul's shoes and they had made the impression on Jenny's abdomen.

The pubic hair recovered from Jenny's body was found to be microscopically different to Jenny's but it was microscopically similar to Paul Hunt's. This was based predominantly on the colour. Clair agreed to carry out further tests before any decision could be made regarding the evidential value in any court case.

The later results however were bad news from Clair Galbraith. The recovered pubic hair had been sent for DNA testing to find out if it had originated from Paul Hunt. The results were not as everyone expected or hoped. The pubic hair, although a microscopic match to Paul Hunt, was not one of his hairs, in fact it was identified on DNA as being one of Jenny's. It was described as a rogue-coloured hair amongst her pubic hairs.

At least the pubic hair had not come from a third unknown source. Clair Galbraith explained that the pubic area is covered with an assortment of pubic hairs of varying shades. From the sample taken from Jenny, none had matched the single pubic hair recovered but under a microscope the hair recovered had looked similar to Paul Hunt's. This had been a coincidence but could now be excluded from the evidence.

Prior to the discovery of DNA, this would have been quite damning evidence against Hunt but luckily the advances in science meant we were able to establish the true source of this pubic hair and not innocently mislead a jury.

Dr Hugh White, the Pathologist had compared the scratches on Jenny's body with those on Paul Hunt. He concluded that they were similar in appearance and consistent with scratches from brambles. He went on to say that because the scratches on Paul Hunt's buttocks were long straight scratches and continuous that they could not have occurred whilst Hunt was wearing clothing. This was a very important finding because it suggested that Paul Hunt had removed his trousers before receiving the scratch. The scratches were not consistent with the explanation of an injury at work as given by Hunt as he claimed he was wearing his trousers when that injury had occurred. It was considered that the scratch was more consistent with Paul Hunt injuring himself whilst not wearing trousers and doing so on bramble bushes such as those found in the den, this would account for his house keys and 38p having been dropped when Hunt lowered his trousers.

The services of the forensic locksmith Mr Crummack were called on once again. This time in relation to the recovered house keys from the copse for comparison against the locks and keys recovered from Hunt's home. Mr Crummack's findings would likely form an important part in any future court case and we were confident that he would make a convincing witness as he had previously been called upon to give expert evidence in court in other murder trials.

Mr Crummack explained in layman's terms that if you look at the profile of any key, you will notice a series of peaks and troughs that are measured using laser equipment and the key is then allocated a five-figure numerical number.

The front door lock, at Hunt's home address RM2, gave a combination reading of 84335 and one of the keys, recovered from the scene 8199AJR5A, gave an identical combination reading. The key and lock had been cut to the same specification. When locks are made however, there are only a limited number of combinations that are manufactured, this can result in as many as 250,000 locks of the same combination being in circulation at any one time, meaning other locks would have the same 84335 specification. It was highly unlikely that someone who came up as a suspect in the enquiry would have a lock at their home address of the same make and combination as the key recovered at the murder scene but not impossible.

Mr Crummack for completeness obtained the laser combination readings of the other three spare front door keys that had been seized from Hunt's address.   IH1, TSA2 and MSP03 all gave a matching combination reading of 84335.

So, what happened exactly when the scene key appeared to fit the front door of Mark Stone's house? When Mr Crummack took the combination readings of Stone's front door lock, he found it to be 74224. He explained that this lock was a cheap lock and the depths of the cuts in the lock were loose. The readings 84335 and 74224 were so similar i.e. the first depth was one less (7 instead of an 8), the second the same depth of 4 and the final three depths were all one less (224 instead of 335), so in fact, we had, by jiggling the key in the lock, been able to pick it with the recovered keys. The coincidence of the cuts being so close was amazing, but the Stone's lock could now be eliminated from the investigation. We could prove forensically that the recovered keys were nothing to do with Mark Stone's home address.

To make these findings easy for a jury to understand, Mr Crummack created graphical images to be handed to the jury when his evidence was given in court.

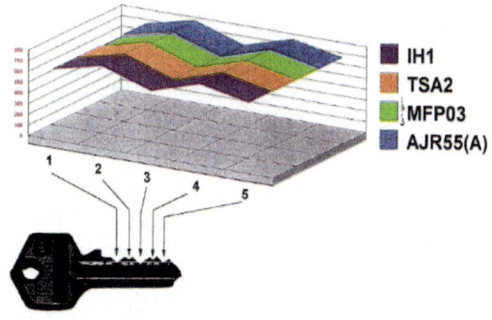

Graph comparison of cuts in keys
IH1, TSA2, MFP03 & 8199AJR55(A)

What was even more damning was the fact that the back door lock when laser tested gave a combination reading of 52625. The testing of the second key 8199AJR5B, recovered from the murder scene gave an identical combination figure 52625. Research showed that this type of lock was made with 500,000 different combinations, making it even more rare than the front door lock. The evidence was building, because Mr Crummack was now saying that the two keys recovered from the murder scene related to two separate locks at Hunt's home, so they had to be his.

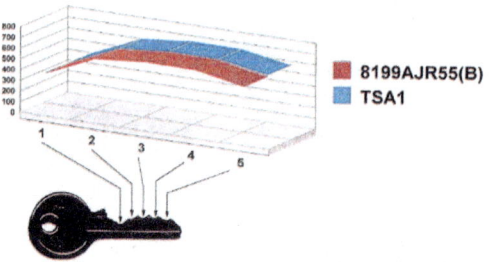

*Graph comparison of cuts in keys
8199AJR55(B) & TSA1*

If anyone was still in any doubt Mr Crummack decided to take his testing even further. He explained that when you get a new key cut from an old key, not only are the depths copied but so is the wear on the key copied. The keys recovered from the scene 8199AJR5A & B were not originals and had been cut from certain other keys. Mr Crummack could show which of the spare keys found at Hunt's house had been used when the new keys 8199AJR5A & B were cut. Paul Hunt had to accept that the keys found at the murder scene were his keys and would have to rely on the jury believing that he lost his keys on the night of the murder, and someone else had picked them up before dropping them at the scene of the crime.

Paul Hunt was interviewed and declined to answer any questions about the night of Jenny's murder. With his solicitor he had prepared a statement which was to be the only explanation he was to give.

82

This statement read:

'I Paul HUNT, make this statement of my own free will. I understand that I do not have to say anything but that it may harm my defence if I do not mention when questioned something, which I later rely on in court. This statement may be given in evidence.

On Friday 30th October 1998, between 8pm and 9pm, I arrived at 'McCluskeys' night club in Bristol city centre. I was with my friend Simon Knight (Pseudonym), I have been going to this club for approximately six weeks. Whilst at the club that night, I drank approximately eight pints of Fosters lager and two single measures of Baileys Irish cream.

On Saturday 31st October 1998, at approximately 1:40am I spoke to Simon. He told me that he would meet me later. I remained on my own for approximately five minutes and then decided to leave the club. When I left, I believe I had at that point, two pounds plus some loose change. A taxi from Bristol city centre to my home address would normally cost no less than ten pounds.

I therefore resigned myself to walking home. I have walked home from Bristol city centre on a number of occasions in the past.

To the best of my recollection, I can give the following route as that which I took home:

From the club, I walked alone through the nearby shopping area onto Old Market, from there, I took Church Road onto Clouds Hill Road, this led me onto Bell Hill Road. At some point, I crossed from the left side to the right side of the road. I then walked onto Two Mile Hill, this led me onto Regent Street and then High Street and then Hill Street. This led me onto Deanery Road. I then recall walking through a subway. This took me onto a path near the rear of the Grange school. I then came onto a housing estate. I went across Tower Lane and passed close to a football pitch. I crossed Tower Road and entered Mill Lane. I took a path off this lane, which took me to Malvern Drive. I live at XXXXXXXXXXXXXX.

As I approached the back door of the house, I looked for my door keys in my trouser pocket. I then discovered that I had lost them. I then realised I was going to have to wake someone up in the house. I looked at my watch and saw the time to be just after 3:30am. I knocked on the door and a little while later my mum answered it. She let me in and I went straight to bed. I remained there until I woke that morning at approximately 10am.

I understand that the police have a pair of shoes recovered from 'Mastershoe' in Bond Street Bristol. On the night in question, I was wearing a pair of black smart shoes, which had been bought for me by my mother approximately 3 months prior. In the days prior to 30th October, my mum had suggested taking the shoes back to the shop because of their poor quality. I now know that she did this on Saturday 31st October 1998, without any prompting from me.

In the days following, I saw a television appeal by the police concerning a set of keys. They looked similar to my keys. In the evening of Tuesday 10th November 1998, I made a telephone call to Crime Stoppers and informed the police that I had lost a set of keys. This was after I had discussed the matter with my family. I did not know Jennifer KING

Signed: P HUNT

Dated 13th November 1998
Time 17:03pm'

Paul HUNT would not answer any further questions and when asked if he had killed Jenny KING he simply replied: "No comment."

What Paul did not mention was that prior to going out on the evening of the murder, he had needed to get his fix from making nuisance phone calls and clocked up 40 phone calls.

We were now satisfied that we had our man and although many further forensic tests were required, we were able to charge Paul Hunt with the murder of Jenny King. He first appeared at North Avon Magistrates court on the 14th of November 1998.

I intend to run through what I consider to be the most damning evidence against Paul Hunt, and this was provided by a Sedimentologist Professor Pye.

Chapter 3:

Professor Pye

Professor Pye set about the task of comparing the soil and fragments found in Paul Hunt's shoes with various other samples seized from the murder scene and surrounding area. Using Paul Hunt's interview statement, we knew the route that Paul Hunt claimed he had taken to walk home. Soil samples were taken from various locations on that route, as well as samples from the areas around his home address and place of work. Professor Pye compared the particle sizes in all samples, particle distribution and chemical composition of the soil as well as looking at any exotic particles.

Professor Pye had been supplied with Paul Hunt's shoes recovered from the returns bin at Mastershoe in Bristol. These shoes had been proven by Ian Steel-Gray to belong to Paul Hunt.

All the soil debris from the tread of the shoes was collected by Professor Pye for close examination.

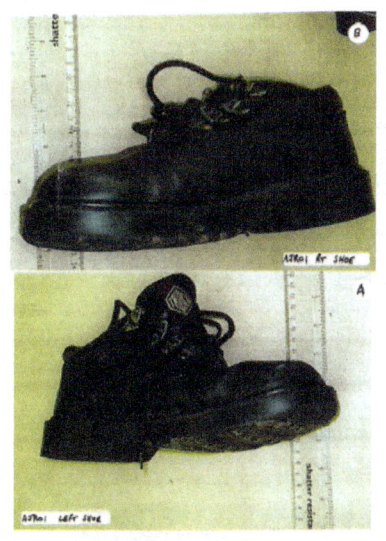

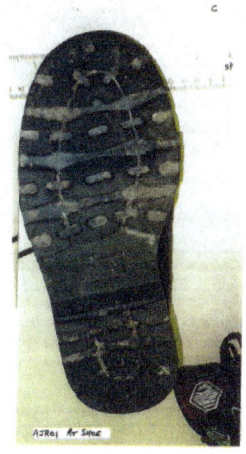

Paul Hunt's Truka shoes

*Worm dropping recovered from
sole of Paul Hunt's Truka shoe*

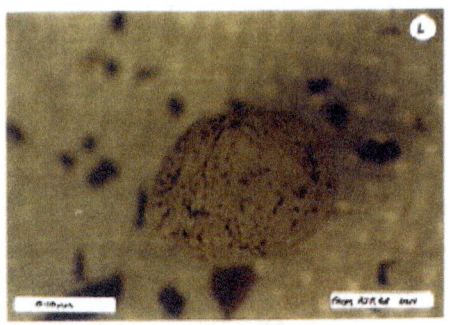

*Worm dropping recovered from
deposition site*

*Moss recovered from sole of
Paul Hunt's Truka shoe*

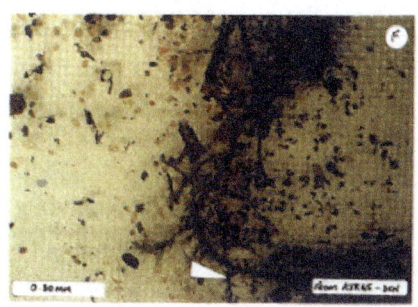

*Moss recovered from
deposition site*

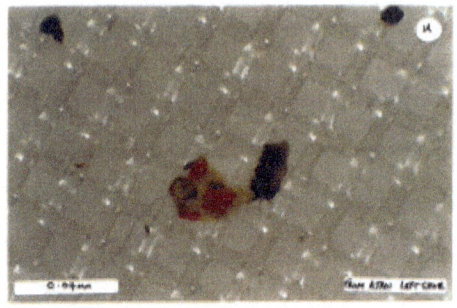

Red paper recovered from sole of Paul Hunt's Truka shoe

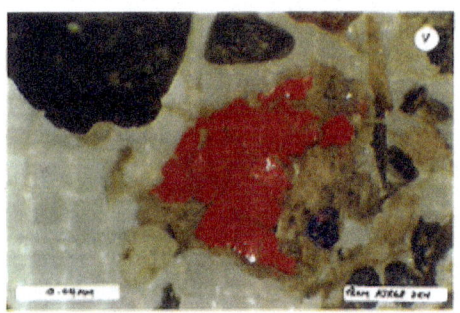

Red paper recovered from deposition site

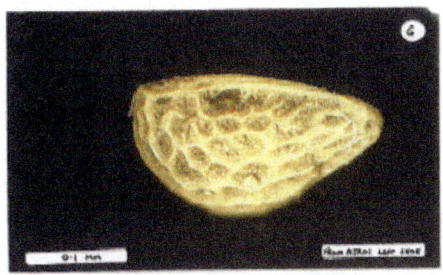

Bramble seed recovered from
sole of Paul Hunt's Truka shoe

Bramble seed recovered from
deposition site

Orange rubber recovered from sole of Paul Hunt's Truka shoe

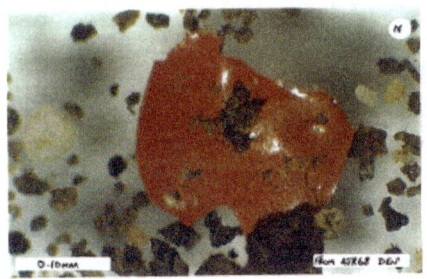

Orange rubber recovered from deposition site

Coloured paper recovered sole of Paul Hunt's Truka shoe

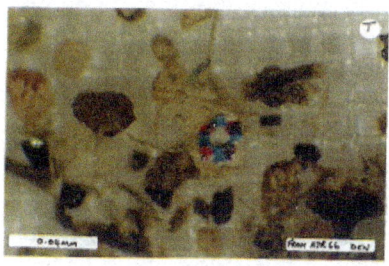

Coloured paper recovered from deposition site

All of Professor Pye's findings showed that the soil found in the tread of the shoes recovered from 'Mastershoe' matched very closely to the soil found in the centre of the den and was dissimilar to any of the other soil samples taken. Professor Pye produced a series of compelling photographs comparing exotic particles found in the shoe tread with similar exotic particles found in the den samples. These included a specific type of moss, bramble seeds, a type of micro-gastropod (mini snail), calcium particle (worm droppings), orange rubber, coloured paper and red paper.

The chemical composition of each of these specific unusual artefacts found in the sole of the shoes were tested and chemically matched those from the crime scene. The similarity of the soils was staggering. The findings were such powerful evidence that Professor Pye was able to show that the soil immediately outside the den was very different from the soil in the centre of the den where Jenny's body had been found. Professor Pye could not only show that the shoes had been in the vicinity of the den but was able to confirm they had been inside the den.

We now had compelling evidence that Paul Hunt's shirt, shoes and house keys had all been at the scene of the murder.

With Paul Hunt not answering any questions in interview, all his friends, family and associates were questioned to establish what, if anything, he had told them. Hunt gave three different accounts to people about the method he got home, telling his girlfriend that he had taken a taxi via Hanham, told his best friend that he had taken a taxi and told his family that he had walked via Kingswood but being very specific that he had walked down the right-hand side of Hill Street. This was no doubt because the press release had indicated that there had been a possible sighting of Jenny King that evening on the left side of Hill Street, being pestered by a young man. One of the last people to see Paul Hunt in McCluckeys was a friend, Lucas Ford (Pseudonym) who stated that at 12:30am, he had seen Hunt with at least £40 in his wallet which contradicted Hunt's explanation that he had walked all the way home as he was out of money. Paul had also told other lies by telling his mother he had recovered his lost keys, when in fact he had retrieved a set of old keys he had given to his girlfriend.

It is possible that Paul Hunt got a taxi part of the way home, stopped to purchase some food and walked the rest of the way home through Kingswood. Only Paul Hunt knows the truth.

Detective Constable Piggott was asked to investigate Paul Hunt's offending history and the apparent habit Hunt had of making numerous nuisance and obscene telephone calls. Constable Piggot established that Hunt started to make indecent calls back in 1992 to a schoolgirl he went to school with, he was cautioned for this by the police. In 1993, he was twice caught exposing himself to ladies whilst travelling on a train between Bristol and Weston-Super-Mare. Hunt was made to attend counselling in sexual behaviour.

In 1994 and again in 1995, he was identified as being responsible for making indecent phone calls to women he knew through work. He was warned about his behaviour. When constable Piggott examined Paul's home telephone bill from March 1998, this showed the concerning habit he had for making obscene and nuisance calls to people. Between March to November 1998, a total of 4,679 telephone calls were made from his home address and at least 74 per cent of these were obscene calls. He had developed a pattern of phoning consecutive telephone numbers to ensure he was not phoning the same person more than once. He had been identified in the past by continuing to phone the same person time and time again and having his number traced so he wanted to make sure he did not make the same mistake again. He would also withhold his number to again ensure he was not identified. Hunt had reached the stage of making 30 to 40 such calls a day. Paul would only speak if a female answered the call and the content of the conversation was mainly heavy breathing and groans. The only times that these calls stopped were on periods that Hunt was away from home on holiday.

On the night of the 30th of October 1998, Hunt had made a series of calls up until 7pm that evening and these stopped when he went out with his friend for the night. Something significant must have happened to Hunt that night (the murder of Jenny perhaps) because he then stopped making any nuisance calls until restarting again on the 6th of November 1998.

Hunt refused to be interviewed about making these phone calls.

With the combined evidence of the fibres, the soil, the scratches, the keys, the footmark, the telephone calls and the lies told by Hunt, it was agreed that there was a strong case against him. On occasions like this, the defence often look for any loophole in the law or to challenge continuity of evidence. The defence had employed the services of a very senior barrister from London.

The prosecution needed someone of a similar standing and used the services of Roderick Denyer and Simon Morgan, who made a formidable team.

The defence made it known that they intended to argue against the inclusion of the telephone evidence as they considered it too prejudicial to Hunt. Bad character evidence was not allowed in 2000 and telling the jury about Hunt's habit of making such calls could result in an argument for a retrial. The prosecution team discussed the evidence that Hunt had changed the habit of a lifetime from the day of the murder by stopping making nuisance phone calls and the fact that he had only resumed some time later. They agreed not to introduce the phone evidence leaving the jury to reach their verdict without the knowledge of Hunt's bad character.

The scene of the murder was in fact due to be demolished to build a new ring road around the southeast of Bristol linking Kingswood to the M4 motorway. The defence had refused to give authority for the crime scene to be released because they wanted their own experts to examine it. This resulted in the construction work on the major ring road being delayed for 9 months at great expense all in the name of justice.

On the week leading up to the trial the defence, at last sent out their own key experts, soil experts and scientists to establish whether they agreed with the findings of the prosecution experts. The defence would normally be expected to serve any of their experts' evidence a week before the trial so the prosecution would be aware who the defence intended to call to refute the prosecution expert witnesses and what evidence was being disputed.

The trial started on the 6th of March 2000 and there was still no news from the defence.

Chapter 4:

The Trial

In March 2000, the witnesses that were called to court to give evidence in person included Jenny's friend, Claire and her brother Andrew, to set the scene and explain the evening's events. Paul Hunt's friends gave evidence to talk through Hunt's movements on that night. Paul's family gave evidence about his arrival home, lies he told, about his journey home and discussions regarding him losing the house keys. They were in an impossible position but stuck close to the statements they had given to the police. Then came a succession of expert witnesses.

The Scenes of Crime Officers described the scene and produced photographs for the jury to see. Ray and Margaret King sobbed in court as the prosecutor showed the jury of eight men and four women photographs of the murder scene and their daughter's body.

The Home Office Pathologist, Hugh White provided the evidence about how Jenny had died and his interpretation of the scratches on Hunt's buttocks that were not consistent with Hunt's explanation for how he got them.

The defence called no one to rebut Hugh White but simply suggested he was wrong to come to the conclusions he had. Hugh could not be budged and that was the first point scored to the prosecution.

The evidence of Clair Galbraith was next. She not only stated that she had found fibres on Jenny's body and clothing that were identical microscopically to those on Paul Hunt's Ralph Lauren shirt, but the material and dye were identical. What was also significant was the fact that the fibres had been up underneath Jenny's top and on the inside of her removed trousers. This eliminated the possibility that the fibres had transferred onto Jenny by some innocent contact between people. The question regarding how common these fibres were never came up. The defence did not call any expert of their own but simply tried to suggest the fibres could have innocently rubbed from one person to another and were innocent transfer of fibres by contact unrelated to the offence making them insignificant. They also tried to question her expertise by pointing out that Clair Galbraith had initially stated the pubic hair appeared to belong to Paul Hunt but was later shown to be wrong. She explained that through a microscope the hair did look like Paul Hunt's pubic hair and were not similar to Jenny's but she had chosen to carryout out further tests before declaring her findings. Clair's evidence was very clear and concise and was another point for the prosecution.

Ian Steel-Gray was the next to give evidence and he was very sure about his findings. He stated that shoes of a type and size of those worn by Paul Hunt had made the mark on Jenny's abdomen, additionally, the mark left on her body showed the same areas of wear as Hunt's shoes recovered from Mastershoe. He had to concede that he could never exclude any other pair of similar shoes, but it was highly unlikely to be another pair and that his evidence should not be looked at in isolation but in combination with all the other findings. He could be absolutely sure that the shoes recovered from Mastershoe were Paul Hunt's.

It was Friday lunchtime and Professor Pye was the next expert to give evidence but before he could start, the defence suddenly served on him four pages of complicated data and findings from their own experts. The Judge was not very pleased and suggested that Mr Pye be given the rest of the afternoon to look over the data and be ready to give evidence on the Monday morning. Furthermore, it was apparent that the data was not complete, so the Judge ordered that all defence material be immediately served on Professor Pye by the end of the day. A quick examination of the data indicated that the defence was going to suggest that the soil on Paul Hunt's shoes was more likely to have come from a large area of waste ground quite near to Hunt's home, where he often walked. That evening, I attended with Professor Pye to visit the area and arrange a series of photographs whilst he took soil samples. Professor Pye on seeing this location immediately said he had no concerns about the defence suggestions and he could easily counter their allegations. He was still satisfied with his original findings. He was however still adamant that other data existed in the defence case. Over the weekend, Professor Pye received a further 40 pages of data from the defence and at 11pm on the Sunday he received a further 12 pages.

Professor Pye stayed up until 2am analysing the data so he would be ready for the Monday morning court hearing. Believe it or not, Professor Pye was handed a final two pages of data only 10 minutes before he was due to give evidence. These were clearly shocking defence tactics, but they did not faze him at all. Professor Pye was brilliant, his presentation of his findings was very impressive. He had a complicated subject to explain to the jury, but he put across his evidence clearly. Professor Pye was able to defend his findings without problem and he was even able to use the defence data to disprove their argument and state how their figures supported his view about the source of the soil. The defence experts were not even experts in the correct field of science as they specialised in pollen.

This was obviously an area that the defence were hoping to make ground but had been woefully unsuccessful. It is always very difficult to know what the jury members are thinking but things were going very much as expected for the prosecution. The underhand defence tactics were to continue.

It was now the turn of the forensic locksmith John Crummack to give his evidence and he was a person that the jury instantly liked.

He is a typical Londoner who appeared very relaxed in the box and spoke quite freely with the barristers. He stuck by his views that, not only did the keys fit the two locks at Paul Hunt's house, but that he could say that certain keys were cut from other keys. The defence experts disagreed with him. The keys did fit the locks, but the defence stated that this was simply coincidence and that the keys would fit numerous locks. They were suggesting that although Paul Hunt lost his keys that night, they were not necessarily the keys recovered at the scene.

Professor Pye

Bristol Crown Court

We had heard a rumour several days earlier that the defence team were intending to introduce some evidence into the trial that would 'blow the case wide open'. This was to be underhand tactic number 2. At the lunch time break, one of the defence team approached me to ask if he could try a key he had, in one of the door locks recovered from Hunt's house. I considered this to be a reasonable request so agreed to this. The key operated the lock and appeared to fit. Mr John Sparrow an investigator from the defence team, was later to make a statement that he had received a call, out of the blue, the previous day from Paul Hunt's mother. She claimed that she had found a house key believing it to be from her original back door and thought it could be one of the keys that Paul had believed he had lost. For some reason, Mr Sparrow decided to try the key in the replacement lock fitted by the police after seizing his original locks. The key fitted that replacement lock.   Why Mr Sparrow then considered that the key may also fit the original lock I have no idea. Were the defence hoping to show that Hunt had not in fact lost his keys on the night of the murder or the fact that many keys fitted the lock meaning the keys from the scene were not necessarily Paul Hunt's lost keys. We suspected foul play and wondered if this was connected to the rumour we had heard several days earlier even though Mr Sparrow was stating he had only learnt the new information the previous day.   What I must concede is that the rumour circulating may have related to something completely different but we never found out what that was.

The defence were now suggesting that the locks were so common that no significance should be placed on the fact that the keys recovered from the crime scene fitted Hunt's front and back doors.   The fact that the recovered keys fitted both locks at Hunt's house was put down as coincidence.   The defence asked the judge to stop the trial and order a retrial in order that enquiries could be made with key manufacturers. The judge decided that she would adjourn until the following morning and reassess the situation then.

We were desperate to avoid any retrial and we had until the following morning to make enquiries to satisfy the judge that the trial should continue.

During that afternoon, the replacement lock that the police had fitted to Hunt's back door was seized and sure enough the keys fitted and were cut to 52625. Bearing in mind we had fitted brand new locks on the Hunt's front and back doors, Mr Crummack was very surprised when he dismantled the lock as it showed obvious signs of having been taken apart previously. Mr Crummack believed that the lock had been tampered with and filed down to make it a 52625 lock. The prosecution now had to decide if they wished to make a big issue of this point and risk to a retrial or if they should concede the point to a degree and continue with the trial. The evidence to date had all gone well and was considered by the prosecution as enough to secure a conviction. It was decided to ignore the tampering of the lock in order to continue with the trial.

I had to travel overnight up to the north of Leicester to get statements from the lock importers. I did not arrive back in Bristol until 3am and was due in court to give evidence at 10am that morning. It was during my enquiries with the importers that I learnt about how frequent locks of the same specification were made. They indicated that if a building contractor was fitting identical doors to all the houses on a large residential estate, it would be quite possible for two houses to have identical locks. The defence were happy with the jury being made aware of these findings and no longer pursued a retrial. The evidence gathered in Leicester satisfied the judge and she too was happy to continue.

I was required that day to give evidence to answer any questions about the investigation and police procedures and decisions.

There was no forensic DNA evidence to show any sexual assault by Hunt, no semen to confirm if the attack was motivated by a sexual need. The only thing supporting a sexual motive was the removal of Jenny's clothing at the time of the attack and the evidence from Huw White that Paul's injuries had been sustained when his trousers had been removed.

Hunt had a history of sexual deviancy with his obscene and nuisance calls, indecent exposures and theft of lady's underwear but the jury would not be aware of this when deciding upon his guilt. There is little doubt that his attack on Jenny was to satisfy his own sexual urges, but most of the supporting evidence never reached the jury.

The prosecution case was closed and it was then the turn of the defence. Paul Hunt did get in the witness box and gave evidence. He continued to state that he had walked all the way home from the town centre and walked through Kingswood and Warmley but had not seen or had any contact with Jenny King. He explained that he originally thought that he had lost his keys on the way home but now with the recently recovered key he was not sure. He had not explained all these facts to the police in interview as he had been advised to say nothing by his solicitor. He denied murdering Jenny King or even knowing her. The most upsetting thing was the way he denied the murder by saying *"If I had killed Jenny, I would admit it and not put her family through all this"*. Knowing him to be guilty and hearing him make such a callous comment was chilling. The rest of the defence case surrounded their soil experts and key experts, but I felt they were less convincing than the prosecution witnesses. The two barristers summed up their cases and the judge summed up all the evidence. The Jury was sent out to consider their verdict at 11am.

It was an agonising 5 ½ hour wait and the team became concerned that the jury would not be able to reach a decision, unanimous or a majority and that would mean the need for a retrial and all witnesses giving their evidence again. The King family had been at court each day and the thought of them having to live through another trial was weighing heavily. Re-trials were known to be prone to eventual not guilty verdicts.

At 4:30pm, the news that the jury were coming back into court was announced.

The court clerk asked the foreman to stand and asked:

"Mr Foreman, please answer this question yes or no, have you reached a verdict that you all agree?"

The foreman replied *"Yes."*

The clerk said: *"Do you find the defendant guilty or not guilty of murder?"*

There was a deadly silence throughout the court until the foreman said *"Guilty."*

Friends and relatives who had attended the trial sobbed and applauded as the jury returned its unanimous verdict at the end of the 12-day trial.

There were cheers of delight and shouts of "You bastard", and it was then that the emotion of the whole situation hit all of those involved. I shook hands with Detective Superintendent Davies, Detective Chief Inspector Anderson and two Detective Constables who had been involved in the case. The investigation had taken over our lives for 16 months. The two prosecution barristers Rod Denyer and Simon Morgan were relieved. Everyone felt totally drained and so pleased that Paul Hunt would be going to prison for a very long time. They were all fighting back the tears of joy and relief. You could even hear the emotion in the judge's voice as she told Hunt that he would be sent to prison for life. The judge requested that a further hearing should be set for her to consider the evidence of Paul Hunt's background of making nuisance telephone calls as she intended to take that into account when making a recommendation as to what minimum sentence Hunt should serve before being able to apply to a parole board for release on licence.

It was to be a month later that the judge heard about Paul Hunt who admitted to making all the telephone calls. Judge Justice Hallett told Hunt: "*Jenny King was a lovely young woman with everything to live for. She died at your hands, tragically young, because she rejected your sexual advances. I also suspect the reason you got close enough to make sexual advances to her was because she recognised you as someone from her childhood, someone she trusted."* She described him as a wicked barefaced liar. The evidence against him was overwhelming and as it mounted up, he had continued to protest his innocence.

Justice Hallett eventually recommended a minimum sentence of 20 years and described Paul Hunt as a very dangerous man that the public had to be protected from. She commended all the officers that had worked on the enquiry.

Everyone involved in the investigation felt proud of the part they had played in the case and how the whole team worked so hard and were so determined to see justice. This was a triumph of good over evil.

Mr and Mrs King, Andrew and Sarah were left to come to terms with their loss, knowing that the evil Paul Hunt has been brought to justice.

Ray King could find no quotable words to express his total contempt for Hunt. He said: *"Jenny has no future; Hunt callously took that away. It is obvious to all who have been present at this trial that he is not just a murderous liar, evil personified. According to the evidence, if it is to be believed, this is a person who within 12 hours of murdering my daughter was playing pool with his mate, and who within 18 hours was out on the town again. He has brought eternal shame on his family and tainted them and his friends with his web of deceit and lies."*

Steve Daly said: *"I'm going home without my girlfriend and he'll never realise how much he has taken away. He'll never realise just what he's done. I loved her, she was everything to me. She was my best friend as well as my girlfriend. She was the happiest girl in the whole world."*

Detective Superintendent Davies said to the media: *"Jenny was a lovely young lady. She was well liked in the community, a vivacious young girl. She was brutally murdered by Hunt because she was in the wrong place at the wrong time."* He said of the period leading up to the murder: *"The callous, ruthless, brutal killer had made thousands of threatening and obscene phone calls to women in the Bristol area, forty of those calls were made just before Paul Hunt had set out on the night he killed Jenny King."*

Five years after his conviction Paul Hunt had still not accepted his guilt, he had spent his time in prison thinking about all the evidence that proved his guilt. He continued being the wicked barefaced liar by writing to the police from his prison cell. I had the letter to assess and in it, Hunt stated he had now decided to tell the truth. I will let you decide what you think about his truth.

Hunt was now claiming that he had in fact walked home on that fateful night and had met Jenny halfway down Hill Street. He knew her by sight and got chatting to her. He stated it was just pleasant banter and he decided to walk her home because she looked lonely. He claimed as he passed the copse in Firework Close (only 200 yards from her getting home), she had said that she needed to go to the toilet. He stood guard at the entrance to the copse whilst she entered. He waited there for quite a while and when she failed to return, he became concerned for her safety and entered the copse to check on her. He found her partially clothed from going to the toilet, she pulled her trousers up and screamed on seeing him. He panicked and held her by the throat to stifle her screams. He claimed that Jenny lost consciousness and fell to the ground. He left her in the copse still alive, breathing and fully dressed. He then turned and started to run home. Almost home, he discovered his keys were missing so he returned to the scene to look for them. When he entered the copse, he found Jenny still on the ground but suggested someone else had been in there and strangled her with her trousers and knickers. Whilst looking for his keys, he accidentally stood on her body, no doubt leaving his shoe impression. He did not locate his keys and returned home.

He was writing the letter because he claimed someone else had murdered Jenny and was still out there free to offend again. Still not able to admit his guilt, it was decided not to respond to his letter.

I had reason to visit Roy and Margaret King in 2011 and they were in the process of writing to the parole board for the second time since Paul Hunt's conviction. Paul Hunt had applied to the parole board for permission to have a home visit in the build-up to release in the future. Mr and Mrs King had spent hours writing to explain the reasons it should not be granted and were prepared to travel to the north of the UK to give their views in person. They still had a corner of their lounge laid out as a shrine to Jenny and her murder was constantly in their thoughts.

The Murder of Patrick Logan 2000

Chapter 1:

The Doyle Family

When I look back now, I suppose it was only to be expected that the Doyle brothers would grow up to become criminals. They were part of the infamous Doyle family from Lucan in County Dublin. The family were travellers that had lived in Southern Ireland for many years. They were known for getting involved in drunken brawls, theft and bare-knuckle fighting. Stealing was a way of life for them, the mix of thieving and fighting was a dangerous combination that would prove to be their downfall.

The Doyles were a large family consisting of five boys and three girls, every one of them quickly became known to the local Garda, initially for petty crime and scuffles, but there was a clear progression into more serious crimes.

This is the story of two of the brothers, John who was born in 1967 and his younger brother Christopher born four years later in 1971. The family lived in the village of Lucan, located roughly 12 km west of Dublin city centre. Coming into the village from the Dublin direction, the first thing you see are trees lining the road, you wouldn't know that you were just a 20-minute drive from Ireland's capital city. The peaceful, picturesque village hid the goings-on in the Doyle household. Their house was a rundown four bedroomed council property. The front and rear gardens were often full of household rubbish including discarded fridges, furniture, and car parts. The neighbours had reported the Doyles to the police and council many times but nothing seemed to be done about it and the relationship between neighbours just got worse.

John's criminal offending started when he was just a child. His father had been sent to prison, so the children were brought up by their mother. John was sent out at the age of seven to steal but God forbid if he ever got caught, because he would receive a clip around the ear for his troubles, for bringing the Garda to the Doyle household. John and Christopher were as thick as thieves and would always be seen together causing whatever mayhem they could.

Once John had reached the age of 17, he had moved up to stealing cars and drove them during the commission of crimes in neighbouring villages. They were inseparable, Christopher would often be out committing crime with his brother rather than attending school.

In June 1984, John and Christopher were travelling around in a stolen Ford Escort car through the village of Clondalkin, 12 km south of Lucan. It was a similar small, quiet countryside village like Lucan. The two brothers toured the town slowly getting more and more drunk from stolen cans of alcohol. They drove around looking for any opportunity to steal property. John suddenly pulled over to the side of the road and told his brother to stay in the car.

84-year-old Matthew Coates, a local pensioner had just collected his pension and was walking towards the local pub to buy a drink. He was walking slowly away from the post office using his walking stick to keep his balance. John would have known it was pension day and that the frail man had already collected his money. John approached but was a little cautious because the walking stick could make quite an effective weapon, and he had to ensure that he had the advantage of surprise. John habitually carried a knife for use in his thieving or fighting. Even before any trouble started, John grabbed the knife handle in his pocket and approached Matthew Coates.

"Give me your money" John shouted aggressively and as he said it, he could see the old man begin to raise his walking stick. Without a second thought, John's knife was out of his pocket and lunging forward. It wasn't there to threaten Matthew Coates to hand over his cash as John immediately stabbed out wildly striking Mr Coates a total of 32 times. It finished as quickly as it started with John walking casually

back to the car and driving back to Lucan. The level of violence was excessive, it was an assault on a stranger in the expectation of getting one week's pension money.

Matthew Coates slumped to the floor and died almost immediately from his injuries. There was nothing the public or ambulance crew could do to help. The Garda attended the scene and began a murder investigation.

Had John not been heard boasting to his friends in a local pub, the Garda would never have identified him as the offender, but knowing his name, the evidence was gathered to prove his guilt. John was given a sentence of just three years because of his age. Christopher was not charged with anything, not even theft of the car. John knew the family rule that you never grass on your family, so he took the rap alone.

Within a few years of getting out of prison, John decided to move away from Ireland. He had become too well known, was getting into trouble too often and the Garda were constantly on his back. John and his partner (I will refer to her as Tracy Anderson), decided to move to England and to set up home in the Hillfields area of Bristol. They soon started a family. He liked large families and would eventually have seven children of his own. The house in Hillfields was a four bedroomed semi-detached council property, not too dissimilar from the property in Lucan. Although John had the chance to start a new life, he was soon back to his bad old ways and out drinking, stealing, fighting and getting a criminal record in the UK.

John would frequently return to southern Ireland to visit his family in Lucan and was always happy to welcome his family to England. It only took a quick ferry across the Irish sea from Holyhead to Dublin followed by a half hour drive the other side and he could be back in Lucan. It never took long before the Garda became aware that he was back in town mixing with his old criminal associates and getting involved in trouble.

The criminal activities of John and Christopher Doyle became well known through intelligence gathered by the Garda. They were criminals who went to recce places before committing their crimes, wanting to reduce the chance of anything going wrong. They would travel throughout Ireland and the UK, normally looking for elderly and vulnerable people to rob. The Doyles identified potential victims anywhere in the country planning to commit their crimes before returning to the safety of their home and families many miles away from the crime.

An example was in 1996, Christopher Doyle travelled to the UK initially to visit his brother John in Bristol. He then chose to visit the south coast looking for suitable elderly vulnerable victims to target. Having identified an 86-year-old lady who was living alone in her warden assisted flat in Bournemouth, he remained watching the premises to understand her daily habits and frequency of visitors. It was only 9pm in the evening when Christopher approached the lady's front door. The flat was in darkness, but he had been watching long enough to know that his victim was inside. He already had an iron bar to force entry to the front door if necessary but when he tried the door handle, he found the door unlocked as he anticipated. Christopher made an initial search of the lounge but found nothing, so he entered the lady's bedroom to confront her. She refused to tell him where her money was kept, and he punched and hit her several times in the head and body. He soon realised that he had gone too far with the beating when his victim lost consciousness. Taking only some cheap jewellery with him, Christopher ran from the premises and drove back to the safety of Bristol to stay with his brother for another week before returning to Ireland.

Three months after the attack, the elderly lady died and there was little doubt that the attack was the primary cause of her death. It was only a matter of weeks later that the police caught up with Christopher Doyle having found his fingerprints in the lady's house. He was arrested in Ireland and charged with manslaughter. Christopher Doyle was jailed for only three years by Bournemouth Crown Court. Maybe he didn't intend to murder her and that was why a murder conviction could not be charged but three years for a career criminal does not appear quite right.

The next crime committed by the Doyle brothers is the one that I got involved in and helped the Garda gather the evidence they required to charge them.

Chapter 2:

The Logan Brothers

Patrick (Paddy) Logan and Peter Logan were two elderly brothers who lived together in Castlejordan, Co Meath, Ireland, where they had farmed since boyhood. The property was getting quite run down but at the ages of 81 and 85 years old, they were still living a happy and quiet life looking after their own cows, calves, sheep, and lambs and owned a good bit of land. They were brothers who had grown closer as each year passed. They did everything together, whether it was caring for their livestock, shopping in Edenderry, ten kilometres away, feeding their numerous cats, visiting the Village Inn for drinks and a chat with the locals or sitting at home watching Coronation Street with their trusty sheep dog Sheppy. The bright yellow farmhouse was located on the outskirts of the village of Castlejordan. It was in the south of the county, close to the border with County Offaly and 55 km due west of Lucan along the M4. The village of Castlejordan only had an area of approximately 2.2 square kilometres, and a population of 85 people.

Paddy and Peter were both in good health and enjoyed the privacy that their isolated house gave them. The house may well have been rundown, but the brothers were reasonably well off, they just didn't like to spend their money.

Chapter 3:

The Robbery

The Doyle brothers' local pub when in Ireland was Courtney's of Lucan and together, they could be seen most evenings drinking with fellow traveller friends getting slowly drunk throughout the night. It was in this bar in January 2000 that John Doyle received a tip-off from another settled traveller about the elderly Logan brothers. He was told about the isolated location of their farm and the fact that they didn't use banks so kept their money in the house. He decided immediately that they would make a good target for him to rob so plans were set in motion. John carried out one quick recce run to learn the layout of the property and was able to see both brothers working with their animals. He was happy that they should make easy targets and planned to do this job on his own. John also checked out the surrounding lanes and located a farm equipment suppliers called P F Gill Limited about one kilometre away, he would use that information as part of his robbery plan. Two days later in the early afternoon, he drove to the farmhouse and parked outside in the lane, concealing his car from both the prying eyes of any passers-by and from the Logan brothers.

The Logan's farmhouse in Castlejordan

John knocked hard on the farmhouse door and within a minute it was answered by Peter. John had already planned his excuses for arriving at the farm unannounced, and with a map in hand, asked Peter how to get to P F Gill Limited. Peter began to give directions but was soon suspicious because the man appeared too keen to enter the house to place his map on the table to write down the instructions. Once Peter had made it clear that the man was not welcome inside the house, the man then asked for a glass of water. John at this point had realised that Peter was no push over and was not going to willingly let anyone into the house, so in the end John had to resort to his usual manner and push his way in, immediately demanding to know the whereabouts of any stashed money. There was no obvious sign of the other brother at this stage and John thought he had been lucky, and the robbery plans had become much more straight forward.

Things soon developed into raised voices and verbal aggression. Unbeknown to John, whilst this was going on, Paddy was in the kitchen and took out his double-barrelled shotgun from the cupboard, loaded it with two cartridges and walked out the back door.

Most farmers in Ireland owned shotguns and the Logans were no different. They had a shotgun certificate and would occasionally shoot vermin on their land. Paddy, now armed, walked to the front of the house and started shouting at the top of his voice "*Get out, Go away*" discharging the shotgun into the air.

John appeared at the front door and could see the red-faced, angry looking Paddy stood there pointing the gun directly at his chest. John quickly made the sensible decision to run off, he may have been handy with his fists and his opponents may have been elderly, but John did not rate his chances against a shotgun. John ran in a direct line towards his car, not looking back yet hoping the second barrel was not going to be fired at him. John heard a second shot being discharged as he got to his car, he jumped in, started the engine and drove away at high speed. He had not planned for that reaction by the Logan brothers and knew he would need a better plan for when he returned. He had already decided that he would not let the incident put him off and if anything, he became more determined to succeed next time but would need to plan better and possibly a brother to help him.

It was five months later that John decided to try to rob the Logans again. John was on another visit to family in Ireland and on this occasion, he had brought Tracy and their seven kids to stay with Christopher, his wife and their six children in a council house in Lucan.

Whilst drinking at a quiet table out the back of Courtney's of Lucan, John explained to Christopher in detail what had gone wrong in his previous robbery attempt at the farmhouse in Castlejordan, that made him even more convinced that the brothers must have a vast sum of money hidden in their farm. Christopher was immediately up for a robbery attempt and put forward several suggestions how they should tackle the robbery differently. Due to their knowledge that the old men were feisty and owned at least one shotgun, they decided that an unannounced approach was necessary rather than a knock at the door. On this occasion, John and Christopher decided that they should arm themselves with baseball bats for protection and to threaten the men right from the beginning. Christopher felt it would also be safer to have a third person with them to act as the getaway driver and to speed up their departure if it was necessary. That person would remain in the car with the engine running.

Rather than steal a car and risk getting caught en-route to the farmhouse or returning from the farm, they decided to use John's car but realised it was imperative to park it up well out of view from the farmhouse. John and Christopher were too greedy to want to share any ill-gotten gains with a third party, so they decided to include their partners in the crime. Tracy would be the getaway driver as the car was technically hers in any case and Christopher's wife would be left to look after the 13 children. Even though she knew what was planned, Tracy agreed to go along without questioning it. Whether she was happy to participate or was doing it through fear of John is anyone's guess.

On Monday the 5th of June, with the 13 children running wild in Christopher's house, the remaining three of them set out together in the white Vauxhall Vectra car, with Tracy driving, John sat in the front passenger seat and Christopher in the rear. It was a warm June evening and they laughed and joked during their 40-minute drive. There was no sign of nerves or worry about the level of violence that may have to be used to overcome the men. It was just another day at work.

On arrival at about 4pm, Tracy very slowly drove down the driveway, it was gravel and she was trying to avoid making any sound to alert the men of their approach. She stopped at the front of the house but reversed back onto a grass area concealing the car behind a bush so no-one inside the farmhouse would be able to see it from within. John and Christopher got out and quietly shut the car doors, collected their baseball bats from the boot and made their way to the front door.

Paddy and Peter were sat in armchairs in the lounge listening on their radio to a bank holiday special GAA Gaelic football match between Laois and Westmeath being played at Tullamore. The two teams were expected to meet again in the local final later that year. Peter had some rice boiling on the stove for them to eat a late meal once the match had finished. John turned the handle on the front door, it swung open quietly, they entered directly into the lounge and casually spoke by asking how the match was going. Peter hardly had time to turn around and neither he or Paddy offered any resistance when John unexpectedly swung his baseball bat and struck Paddy across the head shouting, *"No-one gets away with firing a gun at me, now where's your money."*

Christopher ran across and held Peter down in his seat, punching him in the chest and stomach. As for Paddy, blood was now pouring from his head, he had lost consciousness as he slumped into his chair so he was unable to respond to John's demands. John continued to strike Paddy with the baseball bat several more times in the chest. Peter had gone into shock on seeing his brother's body covered in blood and was in total panic. John searched through Paddy's pockets and found €57 in cash which he pocketed straight away. Christopher searched Peter but found nothing of value. As much as they tried to get Peter to tell them where the rest of the money was kept, it was obvious they would get no help from Peter as he was unable to speak, so they quickly searched the whole house, found no trace of any money stash and left with only €57 profit from their attack.

As they ran from the house, Peter went to the front door just in time to see them speeding away in a white saloon car. Knowing they were gone, and he was safe from further attack, Peter returned to care for his brother and attempted to stem the bleeding. He phoned the emergency services and waited for the ambulance to arrive but knew already that his brother was dead.

Supt Peter Wheeler from Tullamore Garda station was appointed as the senior investigations officer. He attended at the scene with a small team of detectives from the Major Crime Unit. Peter Logan, although still traumatised, was spoken to briefly by detectives to obtain initial information and descriptions to alert colleagues about the dangerous offenders being in the area. After photographs were taken and initial forensic retrievals, Paddy's body was taken away for a pathologist to conduct a post-mortem within the next three hours.

Peter had sustained severe bruising to his face and body and a fractured nose from the vicious attack on him. He was taken to Tullamore General hospital, where from his hospital bed he explained to the Garda what he could remember of the bank holiday attack on himself and his brother. Detective Paul Gilton was given the task of interviewing Peter at the hospital and obtaining a written statement in as much detail as possible.

Peter explained how two men had called to their isolated home about 200 metres from the roadway, they had gained entry by walking in uninvited and were initially enquiring how the match between Laois and Westmeath was going. Because the front door had not been locked, Peter assumed that Sheppy had taken them for friends because he had not barked. Peter gave reasonable descriptions of the men, their car and spoke about the previous attack months earlier. DC Gilton took a 28-page statement before letting Peter take a much-needed break. Although very emotional having witnessed his brother's murder, Peter was determined to be as accurate and detailed in his account so the police would have the best chance of catching the men.

Before leaving the scene, Detective Supt Wheeler had already allocated specific tasks to his team. There were only three houses identified as being close enough to the farm that had to be visited that evening. Constable Sean Gara was asked to take responsibility for house-to-house enquiries. These initial house-to-house enquiries were to be very limited and carried out by Constable Gara alone, but they would be extended to include the whole village during the weeks to follow. Constable Gara would be put in charge of a team of officers later to complete the task. Mr Wheeler briefed the scenes of crime officers giving them specific instructions to examine the scene to recover offender's fingerprints, DNA and clothing fibres. Peter Logan had already mentioned the offender's white saloon car, so Supt Wheeler requested the outside scene be examined for tyre marks and discarded cigarette butts at the location where the car had been parked.

A general observations message for a white saloon car containing three occupants was circulated locally. Roadblocks were set up in the area with the instruction to stop all white saloon cars to ascertain the details of all occupants.

The team was told to meet up again in five hours time, at Endenderry Garda station where they would be based for the duration of the murder investigation.

At 11pm that evening, the whole team of six detectives, one sergeant one Inspector and the Supt gathered at the station. Constable Gara gave an update from the evenings house-to-house which he had virtually completed.

No information was gleaned from the first two houses he visited but there had been no reply at the third property, the occupant it appeared had been in the Castlejordan area at the time of the crime, but he was believed to now be travelling in the Sligo region.

Mr Wheeler allocated Constable Gara with a hand full of actions to be worked on during the next two days and also asked him to collate details of all properties in the Castlejordan postal area so that house-to-house enquiries could be commenced in three days' time. Mr Wheeler was interested in any suspicious people seen on the day of the murder or month leading up to it. He wanted to identify any crimes committed in the area as well as anyone that owned a white saloon car. Constable Gara was told that the one outstanding house from the evening's enquiry needed to be prioritised and he was to report back when it was done.

Detective Patrick Flood was told to make enquiries to identify the vehicle described but it was accepted that there was very little to go on at that stage.

Detective Gilton read through Peter Logan's statement and the team was made aware, for the first time, that one of the attackers had previously tried to rob the Logans at their farm six months earlier. The incident where Paddy had discharged his shotgun had not previously been reported to the police as Paddy had been concerned that he may get into trouble for using his shotgun. Peter Logan stated that he knew one of the offenders was the same as the previous attack as the attacker had referred to the previous shooting before striking his brother Peter claimed that in any case, he recognised him.

Mr Logan was able to give a reasonable description of the two men suggesting one with dark hair and the other red hair, but there were no unusual features that would assist the Garda in identifying the men from descriptions alone. Mr Logan was confident that he would at least be able to identify the man again who had visited on the two occasions and who had killed his brother by beating him with the baseball bat.

Superintendent Wheeler gave an update on the post-mortem findings. It had established that Paddy had died from an accumulation of blood around the heart caused by the rupture of the aortic wall. The blows to his chest had directly caused his death. It was declared a category A murder investigation.

An incident room was set up at the nearby Endenderry Garda station where incident room staff and intelligence staff would collate all evidence gathered and enter it onto a HOLMES (Home Office Large Major Enquiry System) database. The intelligence team was asked to research any potential offenders based on MO and to research anyone identified as a potential suspect.

Peter Wheeler stated the importance of keeping an open mind about the men involved and not to rule out the possibility that more than the two men described were actually involved. He dismissed his team and asked them to meet again at 8am the following day.

The Garda continued with the roadblocks for two days and through the media they appealed for anyone with any information about anyone acting suspiciously between 2pm and 5pm in the vicinity of Castlejordan to contact them.

Endenderry Garda station

Tullamore Garda station

There was just one bouquet of flowers placed at the entrance to the laneway leading to the Logan's home. Peter Logan was inconsolable; he was in a state of disbelief and was finding it difficult to function doing general day-to-day chores. Peter's own face was a bloody mess and taking a long time to heal. Peter had spoken to hospital visitors about the brutal sight of his brother lying dead in a pool of blood on their cottage floor. He was so depressed that he even commented that it was a pity they didn't finish him off as well.

A couple days passed and still bearing the scars of the attack, Peter Logan returned to his home village of Castlejordan to mourn the loss of Paddy. He wore plasters on his face and hands and limped badly as he arrived at the local church, surrounded by family and friends. He had been discharged from Tullamore General Hospital earlier that afternoon. More than 500 people crowded into the church for the funeral and many more stood outside and listened to the ceremony in the rain.

The parish priest, Father Paddy Dillon, offered prayers for the dead man's family and friends. Father Dillon acknowledged the presence of Mr Logan's older brother.

It took another two weeks before Constable Gara was able to report back that he had finally managed to complete the house-to-house at the property close to the farmhouse. Mr Tommy O'Mahoney had returned from his travels in the north of the province and having chatted with his neighbour had learnt for the first time about the murder of Paddy Logan. He stated that he had been walking his dog across fields that run along the approach lane to the Logan's farm at about 5:30pm on the day of the murder when he had seen a white car driving at excessive speed, away from the farm. There were several occupants in the car and the only unusual thing he noticed was that the saloon car was on GB registered index plates.

Patrick Flood was made aware of the developments and changed the direction of his enquiries into the offender's vehicle. He was now well on the trail to identifying the white GB registered saloon car. Enquiries were made for the ferry routes Dublin to Liverpool, Fishguard to Rosslare, Holyhead to Dublin and Pembroke to Rosslare. These appeared to be the most likely ferry routes to take to bring a GB car into Ireland. Patrick checked for travels in each direction going back over a four-week period before and after the attack. He was provided with a list of 43 cars that fitted the criteria. The registration numbers of the vehicles and the driver's details were also supplied. It was then necessary to carryout intelligence research into each of the vehicles, each of the named drivers in a hope of narrowing things down to potential suspects. Patrick Flood took the next week and a half researching but realised that the Irish records were of limited assistance in confirming ownership and usage of cars and that he would require the assistance of the British police all over the UK to progress his enquiries.

Amongst the cars identified within the 43, was a white Vauxhall Vectra R458OEF, registered to Tracy Anderson, with an address in the Hillfields area of Bristol. This address he established was covered by Trinity Road police station, part of the Avon and Somerset police.

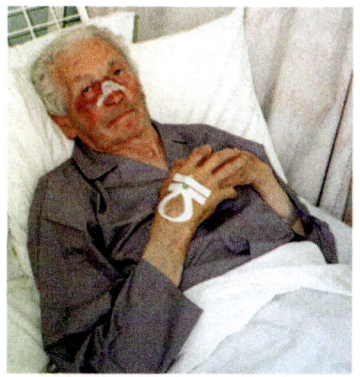

Peter Logan in his hospital bed

White Vauxhall Vectra saloon

On the 11th of July, just over a month into the investigation Patrick flood made a call to Trinity Road CID office to request assistance from them. He may have been unfortunate regarding who he spoke to or simply the fact that

Trinity Road was one of the busiest stations in the force, but Patrick was told that the office was too busy. Patrick then took a chance and phoned the neighbouring district. The phone call was taken by DC Hieron (Himey) at Staplehill CID in Bristol. Patrick Flood was asking for a big favour as he was requesting enquiries to be carried out and a search to be made around the Hillfields area of Bristol. He was aware that this area was in fact covered by the adjacent police station, but Trinity Road detectives had told him they were too busy to assist, and he was hoping Himey would help. Patrick explained the murder to Himey and the fact that they were looking to trace a white Vauxhall Vectra motor car R458OEF that had appeared on a list of white GB registered cars which had returned from Dublin to Holyhead two days after the murder. The car was registered to Tracy Anderson and he supplied Himey with the address in Hillfields. Intelligence officers in the MIR (Major Incident Room) had confirmed that she appeared to live at the address with the voters list showing her as the only adult at the premises, but she had numerous children. Himey consulted with me as I was his supervisor and he wanted authority to make enquiries off district. I agreed to the enquiries being made and in fact offered to go with Himey to make an area search.

We had soon located the Vauxhall Vectra parked on a grass verge outside the premises and reported back to DC Flood at the Garda murder investigation team.

DC Flood explained that they had no direct evidence to link that specific car to the murder scene at that time. He was hoping to identify any possible males that could be linked to Tracy Anderson or her vehicle as there had been two men involved in the murder and a third person driving the car. Himey and I offered to research Tracy Anderson and associates in a hope that it may assist. Patrick informed us that no fingerprints had been found at the murder scene, but this was expected as the victim's brother had stated that both men had been wearing gloves.

Patrick knew that the Vauxhall Vectra R458OEF was in Ireland at the time of the murder and had returned to England a few days later but so had several white GB registered saloon cars. Patrick Flood mentioned that their scenes of crime officers had found tyre impressions at the crime scene where the offender's car had been parked up at the time that the murder had been committed, but there were in fact two or three different tread patterns identified making things difficult to pinpoint a specific brand of tyre.

We started by researching Tracy Anderson and discovered that she had been in a long-term relationship with John Doyle. Although all written records indicated that she lived alone at the address, we were satisfied that John Doyle was living with her and their children. It appeared that he was not shown at the address to facilitate Tracy claiming higher benefits. There were two further avenues of investigation that we decided to take, one was to attempt to establish the tyre manufacture of the tyres on the Vectra in a hope they might match up with tread found at the scene and the second was to carryout surveillance on the car in a hope of identifying John Doyle as a user of it.

Tyre impressions on damp paper

Tyre impressions in mud

John Doyle's previous convictions made interesting reading particularly when we became aware of John's 1984 conviction for murder.

Himey reported back our findings to Patrick Flood and as soon as he heard the name John Doyle, he knew all about the Doyle family's offending history and was more convinced they may have identified their offenders. Himey discussed his intention to try to obtain tyre manufacturer details for them, Patrick agreed but asked that it be done discretely as the Garda did not wish John Doyle to become aware of the police's interest in the car.

The following morning, Ian and I commenced work early and drove down to the address in Hillfields where we located the Vectra parked once again on the public grass verge in front of the house. We could not afford to spend too much time examining the tyres as this would increase the chance of being seen so we made a casual walk past the car, bent down hoping to note the makes and sizes of the tyres but it soon became apparent that the tyres were old and worn and none of the manufacturer's details were visible. We had to think quickly so as we walked a circular route back to our police car, we discussed our options.

We planned to repeat our walk past the car but this time, each of us would attempt to obtain the tread pattern from the two offside tyres that were the furthest away from the house. Having never attempted this in the past, and with no guidance to follow, we had to work out a quick way to do it, and knowing that speed was essential, we thought we should practice on the police car first. Using a blank piece of A4 white paper we tried rubbing it around the tread of the police car tyre. The result was very poor with very little tyre tread visible on the paper. The paper had been too dry and the tyres too clean. I then suggested that if we dampened the paper first it may produce better results. The only source of water we had with us was the windscreen washer fluid, so we sprayed the windscreen with lots of fluid and wiped two new blank pieces of A4 paper onto the wet windscreen. This was the last two pieces of plain A4 paper that we had with us in the car so there was no opportunity to test out our theory first.

Armed with dampened paper we both walked along the pavement, approached the Vectra and, whilst I bent down by the front offside tyre, Himey did the same to the rear offside. Holding the paper on the tyre, we rubbed our free hand over the surface pressing it against the tread. Within seconds we were both walking away from the car holding the evidence we had gathered. Once we had circled the block and returned to the police car, we looked down and were both very pleased with the results of our evidence gathering.

It was immediately clear though that we had recovered two totally different tyre impressions, both were very clear and easy to make out. We were really chuffed that our improvised plan had been so successful. By 9:00am we were emailing the tread patterns to Patrick Flood in order that he could compare them with the patterns found at the crime scene. Lunchtime came and Himey received a telephone call from Patrick Flood of the Garda. It was clear that he was very excited because both the tyre impressions recovered from the Vectra featured at the crime scene and the Garda were now quite satisfied that they could evidentially prove that Tracy Anderson's white Vauxhall Vectra R458OEF could be placed at the crime scene.

Himey and I produced our paper tread patterns into evidence by exhibiting them 3104GJM1 and 2945IDH1. They were photographed, boxed and statements made ready to be read out in a future trial.

Patrick Flood had got authorisation for him and Paul Gilton to travel to the UK to collect the tyre impressions taken by us, but they were asked to also locate the Vauxhall Vectra in a hope of getting tyre impressions overtly. Himey and I met Patrick and Paul at Bristol airport shortly after 7am on the 13th of July.

As we travelled back to Staplehill police station, we decided to do a short detour to drive past the Hillfields address and to our disappointment there was no sign of the Vauxhall Vectra. A search of the surrounding streets also proved fruitless, so we drove to the station to plan our day. Tea, coffee and a bacon roll consumed, we then decided that we would park up in the vicinity of the address in a hope that the vehicle would turn up. Patrick had instructions from his SIO not to approach the address in case John Doyle was there. All four of us were all sat in one police vehicle parked discretely some distance from the house. We had only been there about half an hour when at 10:30 the white Vauxhall Vectra R458OEF arrived and parked in its normal position on the grass verge outside the house. The driver was a female later identified as Tracy Anderson and she was accompanied by three young children. We remained in position for over an hour and with no sign of movement decided to drive to the local supermarket to purchase sandwiches and a drink for lunch. To our horror, when we returned the Vauxhall had gone. We had been hoping to follow Tracy away from the address and with the assistance of uniform officers stop the vehicle to talk to her. Our research had confirmed that Tracy was a disqualified driver so she should not have been driving a car in any case and uniform officers would have good grounds for a vehicle stop.

I knew that two of Tracy's children attended the local school in Fishponds so on the off chance that she was collecting children from school, we headed there. At midday, we sighted R458OEF parked on the road outside the school. There were three children sat in the car and Tracy was seen to approach. We made the decision that we would not allow her to drive off as she was disqualified from driving and would also not be insured to drive. The four of us approached the car and opened the driver's door. DC Flood introduced himself as an officer from the Garda who was investigating the attack of two men in Castlejordan in County Offally in Ireland. He explained that one of the men had died from his injuries and it was therefore a murder investigation. Patrick explained that a white GB registered vehicle had featured in the investigation and that he had been tasked with tracing possible cars for elimination.

He requested that he be allowed to take her car to the local police station at Staplehill for it to be forensically examined. Tracy agreed that this could be done even after it was explained to her that she did not have to consent. Patrick also pointed out that should any evidence be found during the examination; her consent would be sought for that evidence to be permissible in the Irish courts.

Tracy agreed and signed two written consents to that effect, one to satisfy the English legal system and one for the Irish legal system.

Tracy was given a lift home and the car was seized. Avon and Somerset Scenes of Crime Officer Irwin obtained tyre impressions using the more traditional method involving ink and metre long pieces of paper, but Supt Wheeler pointed out that the best evidence rule meant it would be better to seize the whole tyres.

As a precautionary measure, I telephoned Tracy to inform her of our intention to seize all five tyres from the car and replace them with five brand new tyres. She happily agreed to this so the vehicle's five tyres 3104GJM2 - 6 were seized and booked into secure storage to await transfer to Ireland. A search of the vehicle itself had revealed a petrol receipt for the purchase of €50 of petrol from the

Maxol service station in Lucan on the 6th of June 2000. This item was also seized and produced into evidence. At 4:35pm the Vauxhall Vectra was returned to the grass verge outside Tracy's address and the keys were handed back to her. She was informed what had been recovered from the car and appeared very happy with her five newly acquired tyres. Sat on the sofa in the lounge and keeping very quiet was John Doyle, his mere presence would provide further evidence of his links to the car.

It had been a long day so over-night accommodation was found for Patrick Flood and Paul Gilton at the Rambles Hotel in Keynsham. The following morning, they were transported back to Bristol airport for their return flight to Dublin. Arrangements were made for the five car tyres to be taken to Ireland for direct comparison against the crime scene marks.

Three days passed and Patrick Flood was again on the phone to Himey to report that the evidence from the tyres had proven to be 100 per cent definite and there was now no doubt that the Vauxhall Vectra R458OEF was the offender's vehicle. This development was so significant that Supt Peter Wheeler had decided that he now wished to seize the entire vehicle. Himey and I drove to Hillfields and there was no vehicle parked on the grass verge.

We decided to park up and 40 minutes later at 8pm a red Vauxhall Merit estate motor car, pulled up onto the grass verge. Tracy and John Doyle were seen to exit from the vehicle and enter the address. It was obvious that

Tracy had sold the Vauxhall Vectra and was now the proud owner of a Vauxhall Merit.

Within a few hours, we had established that the Vauxhall Vectra R458OEF had been sold part exchange for the Vauxhall Merit at a small car sales premises in Ingleside Road, Kingswood, Bristol. Tracy had got a great deal as her vehicle had five brand new tyres!

The easiest way for the Garda to acquire the Vauxhall Vectra was to purchase it for the asking price from the car sales business in Ingleside Road so this transaction was done by Himey on behalf of the Garda and then a statement was taken from staff regarding the part exchange deal. The Vauxhall Vectra was later conveyed to Ireland and produced as a court exhibit.

On the 20th of July, Himey and I were invited by the Garda to visit their incident room in Endenderry station. We were already considered as members of the team, but Peter Wheeler wanted to introduce us to all the members of the investigation, to visit the crime scene and to discuss the plans for future interviews and arrests of suspects. It was particularly important as half the suspects were resident in Bristol. The Garda knew they would have to work hard over the next couple of months to get into the position of being ready to arrest John and Christopher Doyle for murder and to question Tracy Anderson under caution as well as Christopher's wife.

It was however time to relax and celebrate before the real hard work began. The Garda put on an evening meal for us to attend and the guest of honour was Peter Logan. Peter was so pleased to meet us, the British officers who had played such a major role in the investigation to date, and he wanted to shake our hands and thank us in person. The Garda presented us both with an inscribed pewter plate to show their appreciation.

Pewter plate presented to Himey and I by the Garda

There was lots of planning required and we were tasked with carrying out periodic checks on the Hillfields address, so the Garda could be alerted should Tracy and John Doyle decide to flee the area. Between July and September, new vehicles were constantly seen parked on the grass verge in the spot that Tracy always parked. The vehicles ranged from a red

Mazda in July, a Blue Renault 19 in August and a red Peugeot estate car in September.

The fact that the vehicles were constantly being changed may well have been due to Tracy's disqualification, but John Doyle was no doubt still heavily involved in his criminal activities. We recorded each new sightings of vehicles and submitted them to police intelligence systems as none of the vehicles were registered to either Tracy or John but may feature in crimes elsewhere in the country.

On the 28th of August, Tracy was seen driving the Renault 19 in Hillfields so Himey and I called up the assistance of uniform officers to stop her vehicle and they arrested her for driving whilst disqualified. Whilst she was in custody, Tracy was spoken to by us and she disclosed that John Doyle was in prison in the UK where he was serving a three-year sentence for a burglary and theft of £11 from an elderly couple in Exeter. We confirmed this and it transpired that the elderly couple had been able to take the offender's vehicle registration number as their attacker drove away, the car had been the red Mazda we had circulated on intelligence bulletins. When Devon and Cornwall officers made enquiries about the car, they became aware of the intelligence submitted by Himey, so plotted up on the most likely route the car would take between Exeter and Bristol and it was sighted 15 miles from the burglary driving back to Bristol. Doyle had been arrested, admitted the offence, and sent to prison.

Time was ticking on, and it was now October 2000. The next phase of the investigation was due to commence. The Garda were satisfied that Tracy was not directly linked to the attack on Paddy and Peter Logan even if she had been the driver. She certainly had some questions to answer regarding her car being parked up near to the farmhouse at Castlejordan, Co Meath but she was not considered as a suspect for the murder.

Out of the blue, Tracy made phone contact with Patrick Flood telling him that she wished to come clean about the events in Castlejordan on the 5th of June and wanted to admit her involvement. Patrick explained that he could not talk about the offence over the phone but would travel to Bristol and interview her officially.

A decision was made that it was not necessary that she should be arrested on suspicion of murder but could be interviewed under caution as a voluntary attender with a solicitor present should she wish one. There was a lot of discussion about which caution should be given to Tracy prior to her interview. The interview was due to take place in Bristol so the English caution would afford her the protection it was designed to give. (You do not have to say anything unless you wish to do so but it may harm your defence if you fail to mention something which you later rely upon in court and anything you say may be given in evidence). It was also felt that the Irish caution was relevant because any evidence obtained from the interview would be given in an Irish court. The Irish caution was in line with the old English caution (You do not have to say anything but anything you do say may be given in evidence). There may only be a subtle difference between the two cautions, but it was important that nothing was done to make the interview inadmissible. As Himey and Patrick Flood were going to conduct the interview, it was decided that both cautions would be given to Tracy and it would be explained why this was happening.

On Friday the 13th of October Patrick Flood and Paul Gilton took a flight from Dublin to Bristol and were met at the airport by Himey and I. We travelled directly to Tracy's home address where we were greeted by Tracy and her seven children.

Patrick Flood explained that he was there to see Tracy as the result of her phone call but did not intend to talk to her at the house with all the children present. It was arranged that she would get a baby-sitter at 4pm that day and would then voluntarily attend at Staplehill Police station for interview. It was made clear to Tracy that she would not be under arrest so would be allowed to leave at any time, and once the interview was over, she would be given a lift home. Tracy wanted to explain everything because it had been playing on her mind and she could not live with herself. With John Doyle in prison, she felt able to come clean. Tracy declined to have a solicitor to advise her before or during the interview.

At 4pm as promised, Tracy phoned to say she was free for an interview and to avoid any suggestion of any pre-interview coaching, it was decided to arrange for a taxi to pick her up. Himey and Patrick Flood interviewed Tracy for about 50 minutes, she came across as very honest and wishing to help. She explained that on the 5th of June John Doyle told her that she was needed to drive him and his brother Christopher to an isolated farm in Castlejordan.

All she had to do was park up with the engine running and await their return. She knew what John and Christopher were like and knew that they were intending to rob two elderly men of their life savings. John had told her of his previous attempt when one of the men shot at him and she was quite amused at how brave they had been. John was furious and all worked up, getting Christopher into the same frame of mind. Tracy knew how violent they both could be but was not aware of any planned violence.

She explained to Patrick and Himey, using a plan, exactly where she had parked up and it was only after she had parked the car, that for the first time she saw that they both had baseball bats when they took them from the boot of the car. The two were only gone for about ten minutes she guessed, when they ran back, jumped in the car, and shouted "*Go, go.*" She drove as fast as she could do safely down the narrow side lane and was soon on the motorway back to Lucan where Christopher's wife was looking after all the kids. On the journey back to Lucan, she learnt that John had hit one of the old men in the farmhouse and they were both concerned about how serious it was. They listened to the local news on the television that night and it was reported that one of the brothers had died. Tracy could not say what if anything Christopher's wife knew about the robbery, but she was present afterwards when they listened to the news and talked about it.

John and Tracy decided that it would be best to return to the UK as soon as possible and put as much distance between them and the murder scene. They drove the next morning to Dublin and took the Dublin to Holyhead ferry to the UK. They were back in their Bristol home by the evening. Having heard nothing further they got on with their lives. John spoke with his brother Christopher, and he reassured him everything would blow over as he had heard nothing from the police. The whole thing was forgotten until mid-July when she was spoken to by Patrick Flood and allowed her car to be taken to the police station for forensic examination. Tracy knew then that the police were on to them.

Tracy claimed that John Doyle only hung around for about a month, staying with her in Hillfields, before moving out and taking her red Mazda car with him.

He was still in the Bristol area and would turn up occasionally, but she had no idea where he had been staying. A family friend later told her that John had been arrested for stealing money from an elderly couple in Exeter and was serving a three-year sentence in prison. It was a kind of relief for her that he was inside because he could not harm anyone else.

She was finding it hard to live with herself knowing what John had done whilst she had been sat in the car only metres away. It was for that reason she had contacted Patrick Flood to arrange admitting everything to him.

Tracy was informed that a file would be sent to the Director of Public Prosecution in Ireland and that she would be required to attend to answer to her involvement in the offence. She was then taken home.

The murder investigation team now had the evidence they required to arrest and interview John and Christopher Doyle. As John was in prison and could be located for questioning at any time, they decided that they would next arrest Christopher in Lucan. Once Christopher was in custody, they interviewed his wife, but she stuck with the story that she had no idea of Christopher's involvement in the murder. She had heard about it on the news, but it had not been discussed within the family and John, Christopher or Tracy had not made any admissions in her presence. When Christopher was questioned, he attempted to put all the blame on his brother. He claimed that it was all his brother's idea, and John was determined to carry out the attack in retaliation for being shot at on his previous attempt. Christopher claimed it was only John who had armed himself with a baseball bat and it was John who had killed Paddy Logan. He had decided to ignore the family rule and look after his own interests.

He accused Tracy of trying to spread the blame so it would not look too bad for John. He could not account for Peter's injuries and would only admit to holding Peter Logan back as he felt John would have killed him as well. Christopher was charged with the murder of Paddy Logan and the robbery of Peter Logan as a joint enterprise with his brother John. He was remanded in custody to await trial.

John Doyle was produced from the UK prison to be interviewed. The honour amongst thieves and family honour went out the window as he tried to place all the blame on Christopher. John claimed that when he told Christopher about being shot at by Paddy Logan, it was Christopher who insisted upon teaching him a lesson. Christopher planned the robbery, and it was not until their arrival at the farmhouse that he was aware that Christopher had a baseball bat. John claimed it was Christopher who attacked Paddy Logan and he only restrained Peter Logan to stop his brother attacking him as well. Because the Doyle brothers would not accept the role they had individually played in the attack, both brothers were placed on identification parades. Peter had no problem identifying both and proudly picked them out, explaining who had done what during the murder.

John was charged with murder and robbery and was placed into protective custody in Mountjoy prison spending 23 hours a day in solitary confinement. This was done for his own protection now that the two brothers had fallen out.

Chapter 4:

The Trial

It was not until May 2002 that John Doyle and Christopher Doyle appeared before the Central Criminal Court in Dublin to be tried for murder and robbery. Himey and I were present and ready to give our evidence. Right up until the trial, the Doyles engaged in the 'cut-throat defence' of blaming each other but to everyone's surprise they both offered pleas to manslaughter and robbery, which were accepted by the prosecution.

Peter Logan had to be helped to the stand to give evidence of how his life was destroyed by the killing of his brother. The court heard he sustained a fractured nose in the attack and since then had been on anti-depressants. He also suffered from recurring flashbacks and nightmares. When asked by prosecutor, Mr Tom O'Connell, if he had returned to the family farm since the killing, Peter Logan replied: *"No. I never went out near it."* He moved in with his family away from his farm.

Sentencing John Doyle to 15 years and his brother Christopher to 12 years for the manslaughter, Mr Justice Paul Carney said no sentence he could impose would adequately deal with the horror of this case. The pair were further sentenced to three years for robbery.

Mr Justice Carney said: *"For the sake of €57 (£45) the life of one man was snuffed out and his brother had his destroyed."*

As for Tracy Anderson, she had earlier pleaded guilty to the burglary in connection with the same incident and was sentenced to an 11-month suspended sentence.

Peter Logan said to the media that he thought the sentence was fair but the convicted men ruined his life when they killed his brother Paddy, he would never get over the death of his brother.

The story does not end here though, because in 2013 Christopher Doyle was still in prison. He had earlier been released on parole for the manslaughter offence, but his freedom hadn't lasted long when he received a sentence of three years for stealing a car in Roscrea Co Tipperary and crashing it into several people. He had been returned to custody to serve his sentence and for breaching his parole.

Not being prepared to serve his full sentence, Christopher Doyle escaped custody. It happened when he was granted compassionate escorted leave to visit St James' Hospital in Dublin where his father was very ill.

Believe it or not, it was because of good behaviour in prison that Christopher Doyle had qualified for the prison's training unit which gave him additional privileges and meant that it had been deemed not necessary for him to be handcuffed for the hospital visit. An officer had to remain with him at all times but had chosen to wait outside the father's room during the visit so they were afforded some privacy. There was a toilet located within his father's room and Christopher poked his head out of the door to ask the prison officer permission to use the toilet which was granted. This was all the opportunity Christopher needed as he escaped through the bathroom window. It was five minutes until the escape was discovered by which time Christopher had already stolen a car from outside the hospital and driven at people during his urgency to escape.

Christopher was considered one of Ireland's most dangerous prisoners on the run, the Garda launched a massive nationwide manhunt following his escape.

Two months later Christopher was arrested when shoplifting four cans of beer in a Dealz store in the village of Mullingar, only 65 km from Lucan.

The story of John Doyle also continued, as only one month after his release from Wheatfield prison having served 10 years of his 12-year sentence, he became the focus of the Garda once again when Tracy Anderson reported one of her daughters missing. John had forgiven Tracy for telling all to the police and had persuaded her to move to Ireland to live in order that he could be close to his children. Tracy and John lived separate lives, but Tracy set up home with her children in Lucan so that made John happy.

Tracy feared for her daughter because she was convinced that she had run away to be with her father and knew what John could be like. Tracy was particularly concerned knowing of John Doyle's offending history of violence. John, when contacted by the Garda denied that his 16-year-old daughter was with him. But Tracy was sure that the two were together.

Tracy's daughter and her friend, also missing from home, were eventually located with John Doyle who had no doubt been teaching them the skills of stealing.

Manslaughter 1993

Chapter 1:

The Offence

In English law, manslaughter is a less serious offence than murder. For murder there is a mandatory sentence of life imprisonment with the judge deciding upon how long a person should serve before being considered for release on parole and subject of a life licence. Manslaughter does not have a mandatory life sentence so punishment varies greatly depending on the nature of the crime.

In England and Wales, the usual practice is where possible to charge a person with murder, with the judge or defence able to introduce manslaughter as an option. The jury then decides whether the defendant is guilty or not guilty of either murder or manslaughter.

Manslaughter may be either voluntary or involuntary, depending on whether the accused has the required intent to commit the murder.

Voluntary manslaughter occurs when the defendant puts forward a case that the murder was due to provocation, diminished responsibility or as the result of a suicide pact.

Involuntary manslaughter occurs when the offender has no intention of committing murder but caused the death of another through recklessness or criminal negligence.

This next case was a case of involuntary manslaughter. The victim died whilst asleep in bed and I will lead you through the difficulties of proving who was culpable for the death and the difficulties of showing that gross neglect was the reason for the death.

Chapter 2:

Carbon Monoxide Poisoning

I first need to take you back to the great storm of 1987, which was a violent extratropical cyclone that occurred on the night of 15th –16th October, with hurricane-force winds causing casualties in the UK. I remember that night clearly, it was my daughter's 3rd birthday on 16th October and we had things planned. I woke up to discover every single fence panel surrounding my back garden in Bristol, blown down and strewn across the street. I had to retrieve the panels in pieces and carry out what repairs I could. It took weeks for the damage to be repaired but I had been lucky, compared with others. There were 18 deaths in the UK attributed directly to the storm.

I will be changing the names of all those involved and the address, because it makes no difference to the story, and I don't think any party would benefit from being named.

John and Janet Richardson had been living for many years in their Victorian style 4-bedroom, end of terrace house off Fishponds Road, Bristol. They had brought up all their children in the house, but the kids had now moved away from home and only came back 4 or 5 times a year to stay and visit. Only one bedroom was occupied now, but the other three were there as spare rooms, the smaller bedroom facing the rear was their daughter's room where she would sleep whenever she visited and stayed overnight.

When Mr Richardson woke up on the 16th of October, he went outside to see what damage if any had been caused by the storm. There were tree branches broken in the garden and one fence panel was looking a little ropey. When he walked to the side of the house, he nearly tripped over a pile of broken bricks on the ground. He looked up to his roof and could see that one of his chimneys had partially collapsed and it was part of that chimney stack that was lying at his feet. There was no way he would be climbing on the roof at his age so he and his wife would have to find a builder to sort it out.

It was soon obvious how busy the building trade was following the storm and every firm they phoned were booked up and could not help for at least 6 weeks. Eventually their luck was in, when they phoned Thomas Cronin & Partners of Warmley (This is a totally made-up name and should not be confused with any company of this or any similar name). Mr Cronin was happy to give a quote for the work and if the Richardsons were satisfied with the price, he could start the repairs the following week.

This was before the health and safety regulations required the house to be surrounded by scaffolding to carry out this type of work and Mr Cronin and his brother David visited the Richardsons and clambered up onto the roof using a ladder. They quickly assessed the work required and gave a quote for the job that was agreed. Mr Cronin had pointed out that the chimney stacks were unusually tall and would function equally well if they were rebuilt one foot shorter and in fact, they would then be at a height more in line with most chimneys in the street. The work started four days later and was completed within two days. Happy with the repairs the Richardsons paid the builders, and no problems were experienced when the lounge fire was used to warm up the house during the winter months.

In early 1992 John and Janet moved out of their Fishponds house as it was getting too big for the two of them. They decided to keep the house and following some conversion work, rented it out as student accommodation for up to four students at a time. It was a means of generating an income to subsidise their pensions and they did not expect the property to cause them any concern.

It had now reached the winter of 1992/1993 and four male students had moved into the house at the start of the university year. They were happy-go-lucky lads that were very polite and good tenants that kept the place reasonably tidy for lads of their age. This is the story about one of these students, a 19-year-old lad called Christopher Parsons. His room was the small bedroom that faced the back garden, the same room that had been used by the Richardson's daughter when she stayed. Although the room was small, it had a double bed, wardrobe and a gas fire fitted to the wall to provide a little heat when required.

The students had a few friends round on this particular evening, and they had a couple drinks, whilst listening to music and chatting together. Christopher could feel that he was getting sleepy and told his mates that he was heading off to bed. The time was about midnight and Christopher made his way to his room. It was quite a chilly night, so he lit the gas fire and tucked himself in bed and was soon fast asleep. The other three mates were up by 11am the following morning but there was still no sign of Christopher. One of them went up to Christopher's room and knocked at the door, but when there was no reply, he tried the door handle and found it was unlocked so popped his head inside. The room was warm but not uncomfortably so, but Christopher was lying still in his bed and could not be roused. All the house mates had arrived at this point and realised that Christopher appeared unconscious or dead. They called an ambulance and soon their worst fears were realised when they were told Christopher was deceased. The police arrived and it was them who were tasked with notifying Christopher's parents.

The HSE (Health and Safety Executive) were tasked with leading the investigation into this case to establish how Christopher had died and who, if anyone, was responsible for the death. The post-mortem had concluded that Christopher had died as the result of carbon-monoxide poisoning.

Carbon monoxide is an odourless gas that causes many deaths in the UK each year.

The post-mortem revealed a deep cherry red, flushed skin color, which is the one telltale indicator of carbon monoxide poisoning. It comes from high levels of carboxyhemoglobin in the blood. Unfortunately, with carbon monoxide poisoning the victim quickly loses consciousness and dies after experiencing headaches, weakness or even nausea. It is often only after a postmortem examination that the signs of carbon monoxide are discovered.

Wall gas fire

Blocked flue behind fire

Debris removed from flue

Some of the chimney stacks on the roof

When the forensic scientists examined the gas fire fitted to the wall in Christopher's bedroom, they had a very shocking discovery. The flue that serviced that fire was totally blocked with debris and the top of the chimney had been totally capped off with a paving slab, sealing it shut completely. There was a total of four chimney stacks on the roof and it was only one that was capped in this way.

On the 22nd of March 1993 I first became involved in the case. The HSE had completed their enquiries and submitted a report to the Crown Prosecution Service who had concluded that there was no prospect of a prosecution unless the police conducted a full investigation. The case was allocated to me with no statements or interviews under caution having been done. The incident was months old and I had to now start almost from scratch. I had the photographs that the HSE had taken, the forensic scientist's findings, a report of the Pathologist's findings and a closing report from the HSE Officer summarising his investigation.

I made immediate contact with Christopher Parsons' parents to let them know that a police investigation into their son's death was now being carried out by me and I would regularly update them as enquiries progressed.

I visited John and Janet Richardson and obtained statements from them regarding the work they had carried out on their chimney following the storm in 1987. It was confirmed that it was that chimney that serviced the gas fire in the room where Christopher had died.

To understand more about carbon monoxide poisoning and how it occurs, I sought the expertise of Dr Andy Tubb from the University West of England Applied Sciences department. He was supplied the photographs of the fire, and gas report and then provided me with a statement.

He explained that the gas fire worked off natural gas, which has a chemical formula of CH_4 making it the simplest form of hydrocarbon molecules. When natural gas burns, provided you have sufficient oxygen, the combustion creates harmless carbon dioxide and water.

$$CH4+2(O2) \rightarrow CO2+2(H2O)$$

Natural Gas + 2(Oxygen) = Carbon Dioxide + 2(Water)

The problem comes when you are burning the gas in an enclosed space with restricted oxygen. The reaction for burning can result in the harmful carbon monoxide instead of carbon dioxide.

$$2(CH4)+3(02) \rightarrow 2(CO)+4(H2O)$$

2(Natural Gas) + 3(Oxygen) = 2(Carbon Monoxide) + 4(Water)

Dr Tubb explained that the flue feeding the fire in Christopher's room was clearly blocked by the debris and further blocked by the top of the chimney being capped off. This resulted in there being too little oxygen available for the combustion of natural gas resulting in carbon monoxide rather than the harmless carbon dioxide being produced.

On the 21st of August, I was ready to interview Thomas and David Cronin and I invited them in to Staplehill police station with their solicitor. Neither of them was arrested but they were interviewed under caution and the interview was tape recorded. This was an initial interview to establish what they wished to say about the work they carried out. Each interview lasted about half an hour and they both gave identical accounts, which I can summarise.

They carried out an assessment of the work and decided that the collapsed chimney stack required to be rebuilt but it was not necessary to rebuild it to the original height. Many other chimneys in the street were significantly lower and a reduced chimney stack would function equally well. They both stated that there were several other stacks on the roof that needed no repair. The quote was accepted, and they started the work within days.

They were aware of a fire in the lounge and carried out a smoke test on that fire and could see that it was connected to one of the other stacks on the roof. Neither could recall who they spoke to, but remembered asking Mr or Mrs Richardson if they had any other fires or fire appliances in the house and were told no. They spoke to the Richardsons about building a shorter stack making it less likely to be blown down in a future storm and they notified them that they had capped off one flue which was not in use. They claimed that the Richardsons agreed with them about the work to be carried out and it was finished within a few days. They received full payment for the job and had heard nothing about any problems until they were contacted by me. After the interviews, they were told that enquiries would continue and I may need to speak with them again.

I later visited Mrs Richardson and obtained a second statement from her where she was insistent that she had never had the conversation with the Cronins about whether she had any other fires in the house, because she would have told them about the fire in her daughter's room. She pointed out that she would never have agreed to have a chimney capped off that was connected to an appliance that was usable. Her daughter did occasionally visit and stay in that room after the work had been carried out. They would often turn on the fire in the bedroom to take off the chill from the room but luckily the fire was only ever on for short periods and never overnight.

John Richardson told me the same but was unable to make a statement due to his mental state brought on by the stress and worry since the death on his property. His GP confirmed that John could not cope mentally with the strain of giving evidence in court and if cross examined he could succumb to the pressure of questioning and give unreliable responses. I obtained a written statement from Mr Richardson's GP to explain why it was not in anyone's interests to call him to court.

I submitted a file to the Crown Prosecution Service and they authorised both Thomas and David Cronin to be charged with gross neglect manslaughter. It was recognised right from the beginning that the issue in the trial would be whether we could prove 'gross neglect'.

On the 30th of October 1993, I arrested both Thomas and David Cronin for the offence of manslaughter and neither made a reply after caution. They were charged with the offence and bailed to attend court.

My enquiries continued with scene visits by Dr Andy Tubbs and the defence legal team. I clarified for Dr Tubbs when double glazing had been fitted at the house as this was a point he wished to include in his evidential report.

On Monday the 24th of October, the case started at court number 1 at Bristol Crown Court. The trial lasted three days and most of the expert witness evidence was heard. There was nothing contentious, with most facts being agreed. It was accepted that Christopher Parsons' death was caused by carbon monoxide poisoning. The blocked-up flue and capped chimney were the reasons for the fire producing carbon monoxide. The point in dispute was whether Mr or Mrs Richardson had told the Cronins that there were no other fires or gas appliances in the house.

The defence argued that unless they were able to cross examine John Richardson, the Cronin's would not have a fair trial. The prosecution tried to argue that even if the Cronins had been incorrectly told there were no other fires, it was their responsibility to check before carrying out the work and that by not checking, the Cronins were grossly neglectful.

The Judge unfortunately took the side of the defence, he decided that the case was therefore not proven and instructed the jury to find the defendants not guilty.

Christopher's parents were in court to hear the decision and were left feeling that the legal system had failed them. No-one was being held responsible for the death of their 19-year-old son.

I don't believe there was anything else I could have done, and I know that Mr and Mrs Parsons were grateful that the police had tried to get to the truth. Mr and Mrs Richardson were left thinking that they were being blamed for Christopher's death and the Cronins were happy to push the blame away from themselves.

I will leave you to decide who you feel had the responsibility to ensure the gas fire in Christopher's room could function properly.

Domestic Homicide

Chapter 1:

The Offence

I thought I would next discuss the topic of domestic homicide before giving the details of two such offences that I dealt with as case officer.

Murders normally have a nominated senior CID officer as the Senior Investigating Officer (SIO) but in the case of straight forward domestic homicides a Detective Sergeant will often take the lead.

A domestic homicide is said to be when the death of a person aged 16 or over has or appears to have resulted from violence or neglect by a person they were related to, a person they were or had been in an intimate personal relationship with, or a member of the same household.

The charge is no different from any other murder and the title of domestic homicide was only created to differentiate in compiling crime statistics.

The Home Office figures for the period of the 1st of April 2019 to the 31st of March 2021 show there were 373 domestic homicides recorded by the police in the UK. This being approximately 20% of all homicides. Looking at these figures closer 269 were female victims of homicide and 104 were male victims.

The police recorded 1,500,369 domestic abuse-related incidents and crimes in the year ending March 2022. Of these 589,389 were domestic abuse-related incidents where following investigation the police concluded no notifiable crime was committed. This gives you some idea of the extent of domestic disharmony in the UK made worse during the Covid years.

Domestic homicides tend to display a level of extreme over the top violence caused by a high level of emotion. I intend to lead you through two such crimes, one with a female victim and the second a male victim.

Chapter 2:

The Wife

It was on Monday the 29th of November 1995, I had just finished my lunch break and was busying myself in the office with paperwork when the phone rang on my desk. The control room requested that I attend a suspicious death at 23, Tredegar Road, Fishponds in Bristol. The property was a three bedroomed mid-terraced house, stood outside guarding the front door were Sergeant Sharp and Constable Jones. I arrived at 2:35pm and to avoid any contamination of the scene I decided I had no need to enter the building. The front door was swung open and I could see lying face down in the hallway was the body of a woman in her fifties. She had obvious head injuries and there was a pool of blood on the carpet below her. Her head was closest to the front door with her legs stretched back along the hallway towards the kitchen door. On the floor to her left was a blood-stained vehicle Krook lock with a piece of material wrapped around one end. I confirmed that the woman had already been declared dead by a police surgeon. I requested that Constable Jones commence a written scene log to record anyone that entered the scene from that moment on. I arranged for the Coroner to be notified and requested the attendance of the Home Office Pathologist Hugh White, a senior

Scene of Crime Officer and a Forensic Biologist. I phoned Detective Inspector Chris Gould and asked him to send three detectives to the scene to assist me with house-to-house enquiries.

It was very quickly established that the police had first been called to the scene by Clifford Johnson. He had phoned in to report having attacked his wife Patricia and he believed he had killed her. Clifford Johnson had remained at the house and was immediately arrested for murder once officers arrived. Clifford Johnson was in custody at Staplehill police station. We had identified our victim as being Patricia (Patsy) Elizabeth Johnson born 22.11.42 and our suspect, her husband Clifford Anthony Johnson born 3.11.37. The scene was subjected to several hours of forensic examination and once the Pathologist and Forensic Scientist agreed, the body of Patricia was removed from the house for a post-mortem later that evening. Seized from the scene at that time was the Krook lock and a blood-stained tea towel.

Two experienced detective Constables, Mark Hathaway and Steve Crooke carried out a taped interview with Clifford Johnson to obtain his initial account as to what had happened. Clifford Johnson had a solicitor present and he was cautioned before being interviewed. I will summarise his interview:

He stated that he and his wife had for some time been having marital problems and they argued often. He had never hit his wife before but he believed that she had been trying to poison him. He claimed to often feel unwell after eating food cooked by her at home but he never felt unwell when he ate out. Clifford said that he had arrived home late that afternoon and his wife immediately started an argument. They were shouting at each other and she had then wandered off into the kitchen to make coffee. When he entered the kitchen, he noticed that there were blue granules in the coffee jar which he took as confirmation that she was trying to poison him. The row escalated and his wife had picked up a kitchen knife and held it towards him. Clifford had grabbed his wife and made her drop the knife. He claimed to have punched her once before picking up the first object he could find, a Krook lock and used it to beat her to the ground. He said he completely lost control of himself and struck her several times until she fell unconscious but groaning on the hallway floor. The Krook lock kept slipping in his grasp so he picked up the tea towel, wrapped it around the lock to give him a better grip. He then continued to bludgeon her to death. It was at that moment he came to his senses and phoned the police.

From the explanation given by Mr Johnson, it was likely he was going to either claim self-defence so would be not guilty of any offence:

The common law defence of self-defence applies where the defendant uses necessary, reasonable and proportionate force to defend themselves or another from imminent attack.

Or he would claim diminished responsibility so would only be guilty of manslaughter and not murder:

Diminished responsibility is a partial defence to murder. It means that the accused was suffering from an abnormality of mental functioning, so much so that they were not in control of their actions. If the jury accepted the defence, the murder charge must be downgraded to that of voluntary manslaughter.

What I needed to do was find any evidence that would prove or disprove his version of events. We only had Clifford's account and no independent evidence.

Our enquiries first took us back to the scene where on the kitchen surface we found a coffee jar. Having removed the lid there were clear signs of bright blue grains in amongst the coffee granules. Inside a kitchen cupboard was an old box of rat poison that contained similar blue grains. Forensic testing would later confirm that there was a small quantity of rat poison within the coffee jar. What this did not show was how the granules came to be in the jar. Had Patricia put them there? Had Clifford put them in the jar after killing his wife to set up his defence? What did not seem to make sense is why anyone would leave the poison in the coffee jar rather than place it directly in a cup when making the coffee. There was no sign of any knife lying around where Patricia had been made to drop it. The only knives in the kitchen were clean and stored away in kitchen drawers.

Neighbours and friends all described Patricia as a very loving and religious person who regularly did voluntary work with her local church in St George. She had never mentioned to anyone about her troubled marriage as she was a private lady. No-one believed that she was capable of poisoning her husband. There was evidence from neighbours of frequent rows between Clifford and Patricia but these were limited to verbal rows and no evidence of physical violence. Clifford was known to have a short fuse but no more than that. No-one was identified that Clifford had confided in about his wife trying to poison him.

I attended Patricia's funeral on the 6th of December, the church was full of people keen to talk about how kind Patricia was and how sure they were that she did nothing to justify the attack on her.

The post-mortem established that Patricia had died from multiple head injuries and the Krook lock was the likely weapon. The post-mortem photographs were clearly too graphic to show to any future jury, so Hugh White purchased a model of a head and painted on each of the individual injuries to demonstrate the ferocity of the attack.

The prosecuting barrister was quite satisfied that Clifford Johnson should face a murder charge. The evidence did not support self-defence because even using Clifford's own account, he had no need to defend himself once he had taken the knife away from Patricia. He was not in fear of an imminent attack. The scene suggested that Patricia was heading for the front door at the moment she was forced to the ground so if anything, she was the person in fear of imminent attack. The barrister also agreed that Clifford's diminished responsibility argument was weak because had he been out of control and not responsible for his actions when attacking Patricia, this lack of control ceased the moment he stopped, made the rational decision to use the tea towel to improve his grip and continue with the beating. When Clifford had stopped his initial beating, Patricia was still alive and groaning before he continued to beat her again.

On the 4th of November 1996 a 'voir dire hearing' was put before the Judge at Bristol Crown Court.

A 'voir dire' is a legal hearing where a question of law is decided. It is essentially 'a trial within trial' where matters of evidence are heard by a judge without the presence of a jury.

The only facts under dispute in this case were whether Clifford Johnson was suffering from diminished responsibility at the time of killing Patricia. He accepted he had caused her death by beating her with the Krook lock. The judge was asked to rule on the question of law regarding diminished responsibility. The defence were hoping the judge would rule it was clearly a manslaughter and not murder. If the judge agreed, Clifford Johnson would plead guilty to manslaughter and there would be no need for a trial. Evidence was heard before the judge and he ruled that diminished responsibility was an issue for the jury to decide not him, so a trial date was set. This was an important decision for us because if Johnson was convicted of murder, he would receive a much greater sentence and be subject of a life licence.

On the 11th of November a two-day trial heard the evidence against Clifford Johnson and the jury found him guilty of murder.

Chapter 3:

The Husband

This next offence happened on the 8th of January 2000 and for reasons you will learn later, I will be changing the names of the persons involved as well as the address of the crime.

James and Celia Jones were both aged in their 40's, they had been married for 15 years and their relationship was volatile. They were both alcoholics who would normally have their first drink of the day within two hours of waking up and would continue drinking steadily until they went to bed at night. Neither was very healthy and they were both receiving treatment at their local medical centre for alcohol dependency. They were living together in a one-bedroom flat located in Taylor Close Kingswood, Bristol.

On Saturday the 8th of January 2000, James and Celia returned home from an all-day drinking session and it was James who was the most drunk of the two. The following is the story given by Celia when she was later questioned by the police:

They had been arguing for several hours with her accusing James of having an affair and looking at other women. James slumped down in the lounge armchair and was too drunk to argue any further. He was in fact so drunk that he pissed himself, urinating on the chair. She tried to wake him up but it made him more angry and he swung out trying to hit her. In her heavily drunken state, she reached for a small kitchen knife and stabbed him in the face numerous times whilst he was sat in the armchair trying to get up. She recalls that she was stabbing him so hard that the flimsy kitchen knife broke and she went to search for a second knife to continue. She stabbed him until he collapsed onto the lounge floor and lay there bleeding heavily. Celia realised that there was blood all over the chair and floor. She tried to mop up the lounge carpet with a bowl of water but there was too much there. She had no idea where she got rid of the first broken knife but the second knife, she placed in a pint beer glass on the kitchen surface. Celia then phoned the police.

Celia was arrested for the murder of James and the flat was examined by a Scene of Crime Officer and photographed. A police search team were then used to search the property for any evidence. The badly bent kitchen knife was seized from the beer glass in the kitchen. It was later that the broken knife that Celia had first used was found inside the body of the armchair.

Bent kitchen knife recovered

I was on Rest days on the Saturday and Sunday but received a call to go in to work at 7:00am on Sunday the 9th of January.

Detective Constable Dave Ashwin conducted the interview under caution with Celia and she gave the account that I have already explained. Celia was charged with murder and remanded in custody to await trial whilst enquiries continued with me identified as the case officer.

We were soon to find out that several years earlier Celia and James had had a previous heated argument regarding him looking at other women and on that occasion, Celia had stabbed James in the eye and permanently blinded him in one eye to stop him looking at other women. Lots of evidence was gathered from their friends about the love hate relationship they had and violence that they often showed towards each other. We could not show if James had urinated on the chair before the attack or during the assault but there was clear evidence of the armchair being soaked with urine.

Celia's doctor, with her agreement, was able to confirm the extent of her alcohol dependency.

The post-mortem had shown that James died as the result of 20 stab wounds to his eyes. No other part of his face or body had been attacked so the stabbing was quite directed and not haphazard.

I once again had to consider what potential defences Celia may claim to avoid prosecution for murder.

Voluntary Intoxication is not a defence to a crime as such, but where a person is intoxicated through drink or drugs and commits a crime, the level of intoxication may be such as to prevent the defendant forming the necessary criminal intent of the crime.

Where the defendant has voluntarily put themself in the position of being intoxicated to the extent that they are incapable of forming the mental element of the offence, this will amount to a defence in respect only of a crime of 'specific intent' such as murder.

I had many discussions with the prosecution barrister in this case. He was concerned that since Celia has been diagnosed as being a chronic alcoholic, she was not able to control her drinking so could not help drinking excessively and being intoxicated. In her intoxicated state, she was not able to form the necessary criminal intent to be convicted of murder or the recklessness/gross negligence required for manslaughter. Her blood alcohol levels were shown to be very high at the time the attack had taken place.

The prosecution agency employs lawyers who use a test to decide whether a person should be prosecuted. There must be sufficient evidence for a 'realistic prospect of conviction'. This means that it is more likely than not that the person will be convicted.

The prosecuting barrister in this case felt it was not a question for the jury to decide on her ability to form intent and he believed there was no realistic prospect of a conviction so he decided that the charges against Celia should be withdrawn.

I was very concerned that potentially Celia could be a danger to other people, not the general public, but to anyone she was in a relationship with and jealous of whilst in a state of intoxication. Unfortunately, with the charges being withdrawn, Celia would be released from custody with no conditions. Three days later Celia was released as a free person. It is for this reason I have chosen to protect her identity.

These two cases of domestic homicide have a lot of similarities. The ferocity of the attacks, the fact that both attacks involved a pause in the assault before resuming and the fact that both suspects claimed to be reacting to a threat from the victim. It was the suspects who notified the police of the assault and accepted being responsible for the death of their partner. The decisions made by the barrister were quite different and you may be surprised to know that it was the same prosecuting barrister in each case and he later became a top Crown Court Judge. With one suspect getting the statutory life sentence and the other being released without charge you can see the fine balance between investigations. It is possible that both the decisions made by the barrister involved were correct based on the available facts.

Preview of other books in the series

If you enjoyed reading 'The Murder Detective' then you may also be interested in the other books in the series also written by me 'The Cold Case Detective' and 'The Vice Detective'.

The Cold Case Detective:

Follows me working on nine different stranger rape cold case offences during my years in the Avon and Somerset Police. They are only a few of the many case that I have worked on, but each was different and are fascinating for different reasons.

The rape offences date from 1979 up to 1992 and with the help of forensic science specifically DNA, 6 different offenders are brought to justice. The Cold Case Unit started in 2003 and the investigations all resulted in convictions. I worked on the unit until my retirement in 2020.

The final case is a cold case murder investigation. Melanie Road was walking home alone in Bath in 1984, when she was stabbed to death and sexually assaulted. Her attacker remained free to live his life until 2015 when due to incredible determination and persistence by the police officers involved, Melanie's attacker was arrested. Read how he was identified, and the efforts put in to prove his guilt.

The Vice Detective:

Leads you into the seedy world of prostitution with me investigating and dealing with the problem of kerb crawlers in inner city St Pauls, Bristol. I then investigate a man for running several brothels in Bristol, Weston-Super-Mare and Cheltenham. You will learn how the evidence was gathered to secure a prosecution. You will then take a look into three drugs operations to bring down drug dealers who supplied heroin and cannabis in south Bristol. The case of a cannabis growing facility discovered in a remote location in Bristol and how evidence was gathered to identify those involved. Finally on the subject of greed you will learn about how the police being too impatient to identify offenders blew their chances to identify people printing counterfeit currency.

Dedication

I would like to dedicate this story to my fellow colleagues in the police and the forensic scientists who do their jobs to help the victims' families move forward in their lives.

I would like to thank my niece Camille Leveau for her photographic skills in producing the superb book cover and I wish her well in her future in photography.

I must mention my friend Robert Murphy who is a well-respected journalist who I met many times during my career. It was Robert who encouraged me to write this book and has given me support and guidance throughout.

I would also like to make a mention about the three ladies in my life, Bernie my wife and my two daughters Blandine and Chloe. There have been many occasions during my 40 years police service when I have been absent from home due to working overtime or cancelled rest days. I hope by reading this story they will understand the reasons for my absences. I would never have had the energy and fighting spirit if they had not been so supportive. I also hope that my grandsons Luca, Marco, Renzo, Jacob and Oscar get a chance to read the story when they are older. I would love them to understand the work that their Papou did in the police.

Gary Mason

About the author

I joined the Avon and Somerset police in March 1977 and was posted as a uniform constable to 'B' Division working predominantly on the Knowle West council estate. I was a prolific thief taker and this resulted in me being successful in my application to become a detective constable based at Bishopsworth Police station in 1983. Between 1983 and 1989 I learnt my trade in crime investigation and was involved in several high-profile investigations. In 1985 I got my first taste of murder investigations when I was the exhibits officer in the investigation into the murder of shop owner Royston Page in Bedminster, Bristol. The case was detected with the help of the media (Crimewatch UK) when an appeal was put out to identify a bogus gas official seen in the area at the time of the murder. I carried out duties in the role of an acting sergeant on the CID until my eventual promotion in 1989. For one-year, I again performed uniform duties as a sergeant covering the St Pauls area of Bristol. Drugs and prostitution were the main social problems that the police were required to deal with. The draw of crime investigation was too much and I jumped at the opportunity to return to CID work in 1990 and was posted to Yeovil CID office. The daily travel from Bristol to Yeovil for a whole year proved too much and I was not seeing enough of my family, my wife Bernadette and daughters Blandine and Chloe. I requested to return to Bristol. Between 1991 and 2002, I worked at various CID offices around Bristol, Redland, Southmead, St George and Staplehill and took any opportunity to be seconded to murder investigations where I felt I got the greatest satisfaction. I trained as a scene liaison officer attending murder crime scenes and post-mortems and I became well known for working in major incident rooms using the HOLMES computerised recording system. In October 1998, I was the receiver and case supervisor in one of the Avon and Somerset's largest and most well-known murder investigation, the murder of 22-year-old Jenny King as she walked home from a night club in Kingswood, Bristol. This investigation stirred up a media frenzy which continued until the eventual conviction of Paul Hunt in March 2000. In 2002 the Avon and Somerset police set up a dedicated Major Crime Investigation Unit to investigate all murders in the force area and I was one of 4 detective sergeants selected to be part of this unit. In 2003 the Major Crime Investigation Unit were tasked with setting up a cold case investigation section and I took the lead role in forming a small group of officers and staff to investigate cold case stranger rape offences. I remained working on the MCIU until my retirement after 31 years service in February 2008. With only 2 weeks off, I commenced employment as a crime investigator with the Avon and Somerset police working in their Major Crime Review Team. The MCRT provide support and guidance to senior investigating officers in undetected murders and stranger rape offences and also took on the responsibility of cold case investigations. At the time of writing, I am no longer employed with the police having retired in 2020 after a total of 43 years service. The book contains only a very small number of complex investigations that I worked on.

Printed in Great Britain
by Amazon

45732065R00109